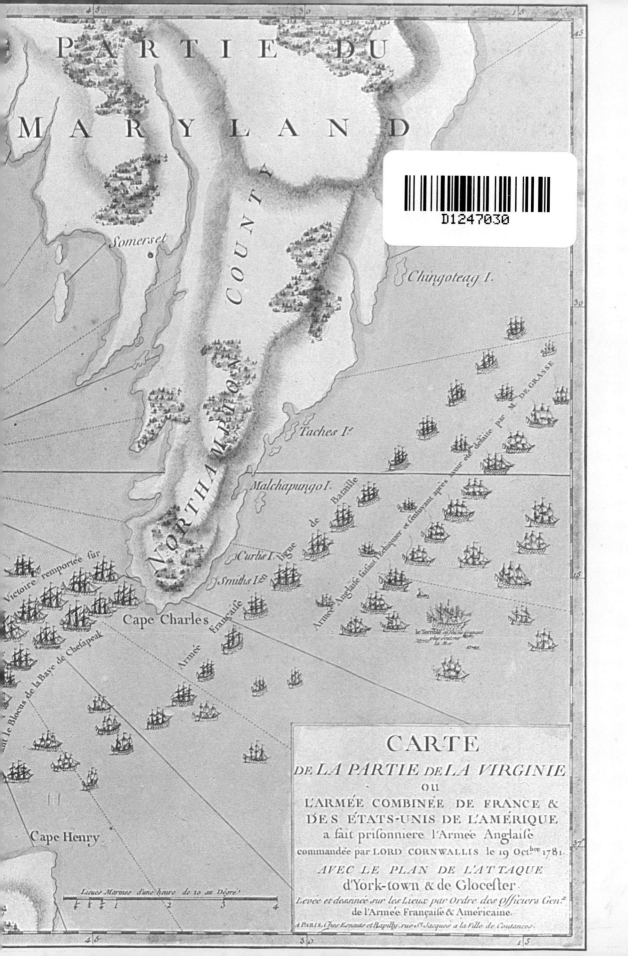

PARTIE DU

MARYLAND

NORTHAMPTON COUNTY

Somerset

Chingoteag I.

Taches I.

Malchapungo I.

Bataille

de

Armée Anglaise faisant Echiquier et s'enfuyant après avoir été batue par M. DE GRASSE

Curtis I. Ligue

Smiths Ien

le Terrible qui s'est noyant plus se rendre à la Mer

Cape Charles

Française

Armée

Victoire remportée sur

Armée

...ant le Blocus de la Baye de Chesapeak

Cape Henry

Lieues Marines d'une heure de 20 au Dégré

1   2   3   4

CARTE
DE LA PARTIE DE LA VIRGINIE
OU
L'ARMÉE COMBINÉE DE FRANCE &
DES ÉTATS-UNIS DE L'AMÉRIQUE
a fait prisonniere l'Armée Angloise
commandée par LORD CORNWALLIS le 19 Oct.bre 1781.
AVEC LE PLAN DE L'ATTAQUE
d'York-town & de Glocester.
Levée et dessinée sur les Lieux par Ordre des Officiers Gen.x
de l'Armée Française & Américaine.
A PARIS, Chez Esnautz et Rapilly, rue St Jacques à la Ville de Coutances.

THE BATTLE OF
YORKTOWN

BY THE EDITORS OF
AMERICAN HERITAGE
The Magazine of History

AUTHOR
THOMAS J. FLEMING

CONSULTANT
FRANCIS S. RONALDS
Former Superintendent,
Morristown National Historical Park

PUBLISHED BY
AMERICAN HERITAGE
PUBLISHING CO., INC.

BOOK TRADE AND INSTITUTIONAL DISTRIBUTION BY
HARPER & ROW

FIRST EDITION
© 1968 by American Heritage Publishing Co., Inc., 551 Fifth
Avenue, New York, New York 10017. All rights reserved under
Berne and Pan-American Copyright Conventions. Library of Con-
gress Catalog Card Number: 68-28247. Trademark AMERICAN
HERITAGE JUNIOR LIBRARY registered United States Patent Office.

FOREWORD

George Washington had just finished what must have been the most satisfying dinner he had ever eaten—one at which he had entertained Brigadier General Charles O'Hara of the British army. It was the evening of October 19, 1781, and General O'Hara, acting for an indisposed Lord Cornwallis, had just surrendered the post at Yorktown. After his guest had departed, Washington dictated a letter to the Continental Congress at Philadelphia:

Sir, I have the Honor to inform Congress, that a Reduction of the British Army under the Command of Lord Cornwallis, is most happily effected. The unremitting Ardor which actuated every Officer and Soldier in the combined Army on this Occasion, has principally led to this Important Event, at an earlier period than my most sanguine Hope had induced me to expect. . . .

The modest, restrained tone of Washington's dispatch masks the true excitement of his announcement: Although no one was quite aware of it at the time, the American victory at Yorktown was the climactic moment of the Revolution, a success that guaranteed independence to the struggling colonies.

Six months earlier, as the author of the following narrative reveals, the prospects for such an American triumph could scarcely have been more bleak. Then, prodded by his French allies, Washington made his historic decision to abandon his watch on Sir Henry Clinton at New York and march south to attack Cornwallis' army in Virginia.

Army life on both sides is amply documented in the illustrations accompanying the text, as is the critical French naval victory over the British that preceded the siege of Yorktown. Detailed eighteenth-century maps show nearly every stage of the battle itself, while the observations of eyewitness artists—and the imaginations of those who only read about it—record the momentous surrender scene. Together, narrative and illustrations present the proud and exciting story that each new generation of Americans will always continue to cherish.

THE EDITORS

Romantic relics of the Revolution, arranged in front of the battle flag of the Thirty-ninth Regiment, include: a brace of Washington's own pistols, a musket, swords, a plumed hat, and a drum.

RIGHT: *Etchings on a Revolutionary powder horn include this detail of the Augustine Moore house (left), where talks were held that led to "Lord Cornwallis' Surrender: 1781" (right).*

COVER: *A detail from Eugene Lami's view (page 96) of an allied attack on a British redoubt.*

FRONT ENDSHEET: *Drawn at Yorktown, this highly schematic French map shows simultaneously: the siege (left), the French blockade (center), and the earlier naval battle (far right).*

TITLE PAGE: *Defeated redcoats march to the surrender site in Van Blarenberghe's 1785 oil.*

BACK ENDSHEET: *French engravers depicted the surrender scene against a tropical backdrop.*

BACK COVER: *An imaginative Revolutionary artist painted French and American flags, siege cannon, and a scowling face on the side of this drum, which was carried throughout the war.*

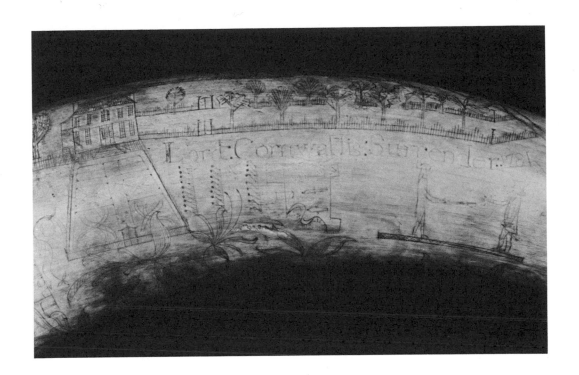

CONTENTS

1
REVOLUTION IN THE BALANCE

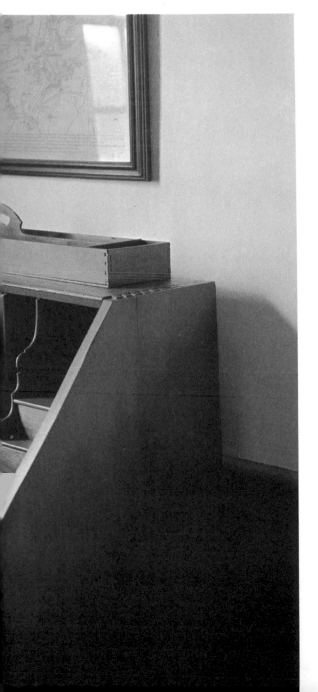

By the spring of 1781, George Washington was the most frustrated man in America. He sat in his headquarters at New Windsor, New York, filling a diary with laments about American corruption and selfishness.

. . . instead of having the prospect of a glorious offensive campaign before us, [we] have a gloomy and bewildered prospect of a defensive one. Chimney corner patriots abound; venality, corruption, prostitution of office for selfish ends, abuse of trust, perversion of funds from a national to a private use, and speculations upon the necessities of the times pervade all interests. . . .

Never, not even in the depths of the black winter at Valley Forge, had the nation's revolutionary spirit sagged so low. After six dreary years, the people were sick of a war that everyone, even Washington, originally had thought would be decided in "a single campaign."

The Continental Army's constantly shifting headquarters moved with Washington. At a series of ordinary desks the General himself kept the Army's accounts (in ledgers like the one at left) and wrote scores of letters appealing for troops and supplies.

The confusion created by the departure of the more-than-5,000-man expeditionary force from Brest in 1780 was recorded by the fleet's official artist, Pierre Ozanne.

The Continental Congress was bankrupt. The paper dollars it had issued in 1776 had succumbed to an almost laughable inflation. A man needed $2,000 to buy a suit of clothes. If he wanted to describe something as worthless, he would say "It's not worth a continental."

For more than two years British armies had rampaged through the South, capturing Savannah and Augusta and subduing Georgia so totally that the colony once more had a royal governor. Charleston, South Carolina, had surrendered on May 12, 1780, and with it went some 3,300 American troops and tons of irreplaceable equipment. That summer the British had smashed another four-thousand-man American army at Camden, South Carolina, annihilating it so completely that they spread mock-

ing handbills reading: "Strayed, Deserted, or Stolen: A Whole Army."

The alliance concluded with France in early 1778 had made the Americans somewhat overconfident, but help from beyond the seas was slow in coming. The arrival of a sizable French expeditionary force at Newport, Rhode Island, in July, 1780, was that year's most promising development.

In January and February, 1781, however, two mutinies had shaken the American army. On May 25, Brigadier General Anthony Wayne suppressed another rebellious outburst in the Pennsylvania Line by executing four ringleaders on the spot. Each month officers resigned by the dozen, and many more enlisted men took the deserter's path to obscurity.

Finally, Washington had to sit idle outside New York while British armies, led first by the traitor Benedict Arnold and then by Charles, Lord Cornwallis, ravaged his home state of Virginia. Not even Mount Vernon

13

seemed safe. He had left his estate on the Potomac River in charge of his cousin Lund Washington, and when a British raider sailed up the Potomac, Lund had humbly gone on board, obeyed British demands for food, and politely asked them to return a number of the plantation's Negroes who had run away to the enemy. Lund's actions may have saved Mount Vernon from being burned—as were other homes in the neighborhood—but Washington nevertheless wrote his overseer a stern rebuke for not showing a proper spirit of independence.

Then came an even more grievous blow. Washington had sent his favorite soldier, the young French volunteer the Marquis de Lafayette, south with 1,200 American regulars to counter the British invasion of Virginia. Late in May, 1781, he sent Lafayette a letter, outlining his plans for the summer. Four thousand men of the French expeditionary force were to march from Newport to join the Americans in an all-out push to expel the British from their headquarters in New York City. The British captured the post rider and learned this closely guarded American secret.

Most ominous of all was the news from Europe. Russia had offered to act as a mediator between the warring powers, and there were strong signs that a peace conference would soon be convened. The only thing the Americans wanted was independence; they would not settle for less. But the British were sure to argue that no one

America, dup'd by a treacherous train,
Now finds she's a Tool both to France and to Spain;
Yet all three united   cant weigh down the Scale;
So the Dutchman jumps in with the hope to prevail.

Ballance of *Power*

By December, 1780, Spain and the Netherlands had joined France in support of the Americans. A contemptuous British view of the alliance, published just nine months before the Battle of Yorktown, shows Spain and France standing over an unhappy Indian maiden, who represents America. Even with Dutch help, they are unable to move a determined, sword-bearing Britannia. The verse beneath urges Americans to renounce the alliance and "with Britons Unite."

THE THEATRE OF WAR in NORTH AMERICA, with the ROADS and A TABLE of the DISTANCES.

Entitled "The Theatre of War in North America," this 1776 map has been shaded to show the extent of British control in 1781—before the Battle of Yorktown. By late summer of that year, Cornwallis' campaign in the South had secured large areas of the key state of Virginia.

16

could expect them to give up those parts of America that they had conquered or could invade at will.

The British possessed the ports and much of the interior of North Carolina, South Carolina, and Georgia. They held New York and Long Island. Occupying the mouth of the Penobscot River, they could argue that they controlled almost all of Maine. Inland they had well-garrisoned forts at Lake Champlain, Niagara Falls, Detroit, and elsewhere, enabling them to claim the area that now includes the states of Minnesota, Wisconsin, northern Illinois, northern Indiana, Michigan, northern Ohio, northwestern New York, and northern Vermont. On the basis of Cornwallis' current invasion, which was all but unopposed, the British might even claim Virginia, richest and largest of all the colonies.

The Americans still controlled most of New England, upstate New York, New Jersey, Pennsylvania, Maryland, and Delaware. To these colonies the British might concede independence—with the sure knowledge that they would not remain free very long as such a surrounded, dismembered nation. It was obvious that the Americans needed a victory—a big, smashing victory—if they were to convince the peace conference in Europe that they had a right to demand independence for all thirteen colonies.

To George Washington the expulsion of the British from New York would be the biggest and best possible victory. He therefore went ahead with

One of a series, this 1784 German engraving shows the French expeditionary force, under Rochambeau, arriving at Newport in 1780.

his plan to attack New York with French support. The British, he reasoned, might think his intercepted letter to Lafayette was a plant, designed to deceive them. Besides, surprise was not a major factor in his plan. To penetrate the bristling network of forts and artillery batteries that the British had planted around Manhattan would take a long, rugged effort.

The French marched down from Newport and joined Washington in a newly laid-out camp at Dobbs Ferry on the banks of the Hudson River early in July.

*Almost as much attention has been devoted to the frame as to the
subject in this water color of members of the French Royal Army.*

The superbly equipped French troops caused vast excitement in the American camp. Their splendid uniforms made the Americans goggle. Rank after rank, they trudged proudly past in their white waistcoats and leggings. The lapels and collar bands of the different regiments varied from crimson to pink to sky blue, green, and yellow. The sergeants sported white plumes in their hats. The grenadiers, the tallest and huskiest soldiers, had red plumes, and the chasseurs, the most alert and fastest moving infantrymen, had green plumes. The artillerists wore long, iron-grey coats with red velvet lapels. The officers, most of them young noblemen, were even more splendidly dressed, and their servants, in silver-fringed tunics and brilliant headdresses, were hard to distinguish from their masters. Most splendid of all was the French cavalry,

led by the flamboyant Duc de Lauzun. Known as a legion, there were four hundred of these hard-drinking adventurers, most of them Germans.

The French, on the other hand, were a little dismayed by the appearance of the American army. After six years of war, they still had no real uniforms, except for the officers, who wore blue coats with buff, white, or red facings. Some Americans wore fringed hunting tunics and linen pants. Others had white cotton uniforms. One French officer expressed special admiration for a Rhode Island regiment, whose membership was three-quarters Negro. He described it as "the most neatly dressed, the best under arms, and the most precise in its maneuvers." But too many of the American soldiers were, in the words of one Frenchman, "almost naked with only some trousers and linen

While the French romanticized (opposite), the British lampooned —with pictures like this one of Rochambeau reviewing his troops.

19

Charles Willson Peale's famous portrait of Washington (right), one of more than twenty similar canvases that the artist and his brother James executed for clients all over the world, shows the General standing amid Hessian flags taken during the Battle of Trenton in 1776. Peale painted many other Revolutionary figures, including Rochambeau, whom he gave (in the unfinished portrait at left) both features and facial expression very similar to Washington's.

jackets, most of them without stockings." But the French noted with pleasure that their new allies kept their guns in good condition and were "very cheerful and healthy in appearance."

One Frenchman was especially disappointed by what he saw when he reviewed the American army. Jean Baptiste Donatien de Vimeur, Comte de Rochambeau, was commander in chief of the French expeditionary force. He was fifty-five years old and a veteran of innumerable battles and sieges against the English and Prussians. He was a well-padded man of middle height with full cheeks and a mouth that was firm as well as friendly; in his eyes there was almost always the hint of a smile. His troops called him Papa.

Surveying the Americans with the eye of a professional soldier, Rochambeau saw at a glance that Washington did not have half the men he had promised he would have in his ranks for the assault on New York. In May the two generals had met at Wethersfield, Connecticut. Washington had said then that he expected to have ten thousand regular troops and all the militia he could gather. Now the mortified American commander had to admit he had only 5,835 regulars and not a single militiaman. This meant that the allied army barely equaled the British numbers in New York. The British had the advantage of fighting from behind entrenchments, backed by batteries of cannon. To Rochambeau it was obvious that Washington would have to change his plans.

The French General was under orders to regard Washington as his commander in chief. He could not tell the American General what to do. He

could only make suggestions. It seemed to him the best alternative was a march to Virginia. Would not a blow struck there simultaneously relieve British pressure on Washington's native state and rescue Lafayette from imminent disaster? "The poor Marquis," as Rochambeau called him, was outnumbered four to one by Cornwallis.

Washington stubbornly insisted on New York. In 1776, the British had driven him out of the city, inflicting two humiliating defeats on the American army. Washington longed to erase these blots on his reputation by reconquering the city. He also dreaded the thought of a march south for more practical reasons. Many of his troops were New Englanders, and they detested the idea of fighting in Virginia's summer heat. Washington feared an order to march south might lead to another mutiny or to mass desertions.

Fortunately, Rochambeau was not only a good general, he was also a shrewd diplomat. He agreed to cooperate with Washington in reconnoitering New York's defenses. Day after day, light infantry and cavalry probed for British weaknesses. They found none. But the two generals and the two armies deepened their mutual admiration and friendship. After one reconnaissance in which they were harassed by heavy British cannon fire, a Rochambeau aide wrote, "I cannot

Vital to the outcome of the war, but generally ignored by Revolutionary historians, was the series of naval clashes between French and British in the West Indies. In another of Ozanne's

insist too strongly how I was surprised by the American army. It is truly incredible that troops almost naked, poorly paid and composed of old men and children and Negroes should behave so well on the march and under fire . . ." As for Washington himself, another aide wrote, "This great man is a thousand times more magnificent and more noble at the head of his army than in any other situation . . ."

Then on August 12 came a blow from an unexpected direction. A fleet of twenty British ships stood into New York harbor. Washington's spies soon informed him that they carried fifteen hundred reinforcements from Europe —enough to bring British numbers in New York above those of their would-be attackers. Once more Rochambeau seized the opportunity to urge a march to Virginia. Still Washington wavered, although by now it was evident from his diary that he had given up any real hope of capturing New York. The most he yearned to do now was to find a place most favorable to "a partisan stroke."

While Rochambeau conferred with Washington, the French commander carried on a fateful correspondence with another Frenchman. Comte François Joseph Paul de Grasse, Marquis de Grasse-Tilly, was the admiral in command of the French West Indies fleet. He was under orders to

drawings (above), French admirals d'Estaing and de Grasse capture St. George. From such an outpost, the French fleet that set up the crucial blockade of Yorktown was launched.

With almost 30,000 German mercenaries on the British army's payroll, the war itself was a topic of great interest in Germany—where this illustration served as a peepshow backdrop. Royal forces march into a highly fanciful New York of 1776 that includes Trinity Church (center background) with its steeple—which actually had been destroyed earlier that year—still intact.

spend a very limited amount of time—no more than a month—in American waters during late August or September, co-operating with Washington and Rochambeau. No attack on New York could succeed without the help of a superior fleet, and Washington had included Admiral de Grasse's presence in his plans to capture the city. When American recruitment failed to bring his army up to strength,

peake Bay. Virginia, he wrote, "is where we think you may be able to render the greatest service."

On August 14, a messenger came pounding into the allied camp from Newport. One of de Grasse's frigates (fast, light ships, the destroyers of their day) had just arrived at the French base there with word that the Admiral was en route to the Chesapeake and that he was bringing with him twenty-nine warships and three thousand soldiers.

Once more Rochambeau pressed Washington for a decision to march south. Reluctantly the American commander in chief agreed. But at this point Washington did not believe that Cornwallis and his army would still be in Virginia when the French and Americans arrived. Basing his conclusion on previous experience, he assumed that the British would retreat to the coast. Cornwallis would leave only a detachment there and send the rest of his army either to New York or to South Carolina, where another American army under General Nathanael Greene was threatening scattered British posts. Washington stated this opinion twice, in letters to his stepson Jack Custis and to Lafayette.

Then on August 17 came a dispatch from Lafayette with news that changed everything. Lord Cornwallis had retreated to the small tobacco port of York near the mouth of the river with the same name. He was using his whole army to fortify the place. There was no time to be lost!

Washington had suggested that the Admiral might bring with him more French troops from the West Indies. But de Grasse, out of touch with the American situation during his long voyage from France, depended on Rochambeau to advise him where his men and guns would be most useful.

In a series of letters, Rochambeau discreetly steered the Admiral away from New York and toward Chesa-

2

THE BRITISH DIVIDED

Behind his New York fortifications, the British commander in chief in America, Sir Henry Clinton, was almost as frustrated as George Washington. His letters to his superiors in London were one long wail about lack of troops, lack of supplies, lack of wagons, lack of horses, lack of ships. To all who would listen he complained, "The idea in England is that I keep a great army here and yet it is nearly equally divided between New York, Virginia and South Carolina."

A rather fat, moon-faced man, Clinton had come to America in 1775 with major generals Sir William Howe and John Burgoyne. He had seen Burgoyne captured at Saratoga, and he had seen Howe resign in frustration when the government failed to send him the troops that he felt he needed to end the rebellion.

Just after Clinton succeeded Howe to the supreme command, the French entered the war, and the British decided to abandon Philadelphia and concentrate their army in New York. Under orders, Clinton was forced to send 5,800 of his troops to the West Indies. As France attacked England around the world—in India, Africa, and the West Indies—and threatened the coast of England itself, it became more and more difficult for the government to give Clinton the men he now insisted that he needed.

Clinton was a perfectionist. If he felt that any part of his equipment or supplies for a campaign was less than ideal, he preferred to do nothing. George Sackville, Lord Germain, Secretary of State for Colonies and the man responsible for planning the war from London, soon became disillusioned with Clinton. "I expect little exertion from that quarter," he wrote glumly to an associate. Yet Lord Germain could not force Clinton to resign. Thanks to some influential friends in the British court, this do-little commander was one of George III's favorite generals.

Sir Henry Clinton's life in old Manhattan must have been a pleasant one. He had, according to one account, four houses, including a comfortable mansion in town and a country manor on Long Island. But around

Sir Henry Clinton, commander in chief of British forces in North America in 1781.

him were gathered some of the worst characters in the history of the British army, and Clinton did nothing to stop their looting and grafting. His second in command was Major General James Robertson, a sly manipulator who had a large personal interest in the firm that sold supplies to the British army. Another rascal was Brigadier General Samuel Birch, who plundered rebels and loyalists indiscriminately.

From December 31, 1775, to May 16, 1778, the British army under the command of Sir William Howe spent £1,079,412. But between May 26, 1778, and December 31, 1780, under Sir Henry Clinton's regime, a somewhat smaller army spent £3,278,429 —nearly three times as much in approximately the same length of time. A board of inquiry was appointed by Sir Henry to find out why but did not even manage to turn up a decent explanation. This was hardly surprising. The members of the board were all army officers, and many of them were probably up to their elbows in the very graft they were investigating.

Clinton's inertia was unintentionally encouraged by the man who acted as his spymaster. He was William Smith, an American-born loyalist who constantly gave Clinton evidence— which he had no trouble finding—that the American rebellion was close to collapse. But Sir Henry did not accept Smith's conclusion—one solid blow by the British army and the war would be over. Instead, Sir Henry decided that the best way to win was to sit tight in fortified New York and let the rebels wither away outside.

Unfortunately for Sir Henry and for Great Britain, this idea was never successfully communicated to Lord Cornwallis. After directing the capture of Charleston in May, 1780, Clinton had returned to New York and left Cornwallis in charge of operations in the South. He gave him what he considered an ample army and ordered him to concentrate on subduing South Carolina and maintaining the already

Ambitious and overoptimistic, Cornwallis (shown above in a 1781 English engraving) ignored Clinton's orders to secure South Carolina and instead marched into Virginia.

A British garrison through most of the war, New York in 1778 was considerably less tranquil than this wash drawing indicates. British troops had been quartered in the city since Howe's humiliating expulsion of Washington's forces in August, 1776. Their presence made Manhattan a source of political embarrassment to the allies, as well as a prime military objective.

firm British grip on Georgia. Although he was the same age as Clinton—forty-three—Cornwallis seemed years younger than the paunchy commander in chief. He was a lean, rather hawk-nosed man, and an aggressive fighter, as he had proved on a half-dozen Revolutionary battlefields. He was, moreover, the descendant of an old and distinguished English family, with far more hereditary prestige than Clinton.

The combination inclined Cornwallis not only to dislike Clinton's passive strategy, but to do something about it as well. With the excuse that Clinton was too far away in New York to confer on strategy, Cornwallis wangled authority to communicate directly with London. He briskly set about occupying the interior of South Carolina and setting up British outposts at strategic points. His annihilation of the American army led by Horatio Gates at Camden, South Carolina, on August 16, 1780, was such a total victory that it inspired

29

Slow and uncertain communication with the Colonies made it difficult for the British Board of the Admiralty (depicted above by the eighteenth-century caricaturist Thomas Rowlandson) to advise its overseas commanders. In the Colonies, similar delays and confusion allowed Cornwallis to disregard Clinton's directives and pursue a virtually independent strategy.

Cornwallis to move into North Carolina. He hoped that the loyalists there would rise en masse to support him.

But the Americans were merely down, not out. Over a thousand loyalists who responded to the British call were annihilated in turn by American irregulars at Kings Mountain, South Carolina, on October 7, 1780. When Cornwallis detached his cavalry leader, Colonel Banastre Tarleton, and a corps of crack troops to attack a small patriot army under General Daniel Morgan, they too were all but destroyed, at the battle of Cowpens, South Carolina, on January 17, 1781.

Two months later, on March 15, Cornwallis himself fought a brutal seesaw struggle with a reinforced American army under Nathanael Greene at Guilford Court House, North Carolina. In a desperate day-long fight, Cornwallis drove the Americans from the field, but he paid a terrible price. The victorious British army staggered back to Wilmington, on North Carolina's coast, with less than a thousand men fit for duty and a wagon train carrying twice that number of sick and wounded.

By then Cornwallis too was a frustrated man. He told the new British commander in Virginia, Major General William Phillips, that he was "quite tired of marching about the country in quest of adventures." After studying his map, Cornwallis decided that Virginia was the key to the war. From this, the oldest, richest, proudest, most populated of the rebellious colonies, had come the reinforcements and supplies that enabled the Americans to replace their defeated southern armies so tirelessly.

After reinforcing his decimated battalions from Charleston, Cornwallis wrote Phillips that he was planning to join him in Virginia. Another letter informed Lord Germain of his intentions. But curiously, Cornwallis did not bother to tell his nominal superior, Sir Henry Clinton, what he was going to do until April 23, the day before he began his march north.

This omission is the best evidence of the divided state of the British high command. Clinton's reaction to the news of Cornwallis' move made the rift between the two men even more apparent. The British commander in chief dispatched a cranky, disapproving letter: ". . . had it been possible . . . for Your Lordship to have let me know your views and intentions, I should not now be at a loss to judge of the force you might want for your operations." As Cornwallis raided deep into Virginia, the two generals began a barely polite argument by correspondence about how to win the war. Then Clinton ordered Cornwallis to withdraw to the coast and send almost half his army to New York.

OVERLEAF: *Forced to stand and fight at Cowpens, South Carolina, in January, 1781, Daniel Morgan's well-hidden Americans dealt a detachment of Cornwallis' army the worst British defeat since Saratoga. William Ranney painted the cavalry clash.*

Germain, Secretary of State for Colonies

When Cornwallis received this letter, he became bitterly disgusted. For well over a month, he had been moving at will through Virginia, burning tons of tobacco, grain, and corn, slaughtering thousands of horses and cattle, even sending Governor Thomas Jefferson and the members of the Virginia Assembly fleeing into the woods like common fugitives to escape his cavalry. Lafayette and his twelve hundred Continentals were helpless. They could only watch from a wary distance, hoping that a part of the British army might drop its guard and give them a chance to attack. Cornwallis was doing exactly what he hoped— smashing Virginia's will to resist.

Now, obedient to orders, he had to abandon his plan and retreat toward the coast, with Lafayette nipping at his heels, doing his best to make it look as if his meager little band of Continentals was actually forcing the big British army to run away. On July 6, Lafayette, reinforced by nine hundred Pennsylvanians, tried to attack Cornwallis at Green Spring Plantation, where the British army was crossing the James River.

Cornwallis showed his superior generalship by luring the young Frenchman into a nearly fatal trap. Instead of ordering his entire army across the river and leaving only a rear guard on the nearest shore, Cornwallis sent only a single regiment across, with orders to light enough campfires on the far shore to make it look as if the entire army was there.

Lafayette sprang at the bait and attacked what he thought was the rear guard. Out of the woods rumbled the main British army, to send the Marquis and his startled Americans into frantic retreat. A vigorous pursuit by Cornwallis might have annihilated the little American army. But Cornwallis felt that his orders from Clinton forbade him to make the effort.

Although he obeyed Clinton's orders, Cornwallis did not hesitate to remind his superior in New York that Lord Germain had approved the operations in Virginia. Back and forth went more irritable letters between the two generals. Finally, Clinton tried to compromise. He ordered Cornwallis to create a fortified post on the Virginia coast from which more ambitious operations could be launched later in the year. After more quibbling and quarreling over a location, Cornwallis impatiently chose the port of York and the small settlement directly across the York River from it, Gloucester. By now Cornwallis was so disgusted with Clinton that he became more than a little vindictive. In order to do an adequate job of fortifying the town, Cornwallis insisted that he would have to retain every one of the 8,885 soldiers under his command.

Late in July, Cornwallis led the 80th Infantry Regiment aboard transports in Portsmouth harbor. Uncooperative winds kept them at sea in the broad mouth of Chesapeake Bay for four days, but on August 2 he saw

Cornwallis Retreating !

PHILADELPHIA, April 7, 1781.

Extract of a Letter from Major-General *Greene*, dated CAMP, at *Buffelo Creek, March* 23, 1781.

"ON the 16th Inftant I wrote your Excellency, giving an Account of an Action which happened at Guilford Court-Houfe the Day before. I was then perfuaded that notwithftanding we were obliged to give up the Ground, we had reaped the Advantage of the Action. Circumftances fince confirm me in Opinion that the Enemy were too much gauled to improve their Succefs. We lay at the Iron-Works three Days, preparing ourfelves for another Action, and expecting the Enemy to advance : But of a fudden they took their Departure, leaving behind them evident Marks of Diftrefs. All our wounded at Guilford, which had fallen into their Hands, and 70 of their own, too bad to move, were left at New-Garden. Moft of their Officers fuffered-- Lord Cornwallis had his Horfe fhot under him--- Col. Steward, of the Guards was killed, General O Hara and Cols, Tarlton and Webfter, wounded. Only three Field-Officers efcaped, if Reports, which feem to be authentic, can be relied on.

Our Army are in good Spirits, notwithftanding our Sufferings, and are advancing towards the Enemy; they are retreating to Crofs-Creek.

In South-Carolina, Generals Sumpter and Marian have gained feveral little Advantages. In one the Enemy loft 60 Men, who had under their Care a large Quantity of Stores, which were taken, but by an unfortunate Miftake were afterwards re taken.

Publifhed by Order,

CHARLES THOMSON, Secretary.

§†§ Printed at N. Willis's Office.

The news from Virginia was indeed too good to be true. Despite heavy losses at Guilford Court House in March, 1781, Cornwallis was withdrawing—not retreating—to York.

the town of York dozing in the humid morning heat. There was a cluster of about sixty houses down on the riverside and another two hundred fifty residences on the thirty-five-foot-high bluffs above. About three hundred Virginia militiamen were stationed in the town, but the sight of the British ships sent them scampering back to Williamsburg, fourteen miles away, at the opposite end of the peninsula.

Until 1750, Yorktown had been the busiest tobacco port on the Chesapeake. The merchants and shippers who lived there built themselves houses that one European traveler declared equal in magnificence to many in England. In the decade before the Revolution other ports took over the tobacco trade and Yorktown declined, but the rich houses remained.

For his headquarters, Cornwallis selected the finest house in town. It was owned by Thomas Nelson, former secretary of the Virginia legislature. The house was a handsome two-story red brick affair, decorated inside in the latest English taste. Nelson had remained neutral throughout the war, and Cornwallis treated him with the utmost courtesy.

Cornwallis' attitude toward Yorktown, from a military point of view, is evident in the letter he wrote to his second in command, Brigadier General Charles O'Hara: "After a passage of four days we landed here and at Gloucester without opposition. The position is bad and of course we want more troops. . . ."

Yorktown in 1755 was one of the busiest tobacco ports on the Chesapeake. Each year hundreds of hogsheads of dried, bundled leaves were loaded from the local wharves (which are unaccountably missing in this sketch by an unknown

British naval officer). By August, 1781, when Cornwallis and his army reached the city, its importance as a trading center had sharply declined, although its handsome houses—one of which became Cornwallis' headquarters—remained.

37

3

THE GRAND DECEPTION

While Cornwallis and his men toiled in the scorching Virginia sun to make Yorktown's bad position defensible, Washington and Rochambeau planned their march south. Washington sent letters to state governors, begging them once more for recruits to fill up the regiments that would be left to guard the Hudson River. Robert Morris, superintendent of American finance, was told to hire ships on credit to transport the infantry from Philadelphia to Virginia, and also to raise, somehow, enough hard money to pay the troops one month's wages. Another express rider rode north with a message for Admiral Comte de Barras, who commanded the French base at Newport.

Barras was guarding the French heavy artillery that was absolutely necessary to conduct a successful siege. He was also sitting on 1,500 tons of salt beef, reserve provisions of the French army. The two generals calculated that they would badly need these provisions to feed the mass of men they were concentrating in Virginia. Would the Admiral kindly put

the guns and groceries aboard his ships, Washington and Rochambeau wrote, and rendezvous with them in Virginia?

Admiral Barras decided he would most kindly do no such thing. He was unhappy because Admiral de Grasse's West Indies fleet of twenty-nine ships would outnumber his eight. Not only was de Grasse the junior of the two by several years; he had even served once under Barras as a cadet. Admiral Barras simply could not accept a position in which he would have to receive orders from his former subordinate. To avoid such embarrassment, he planned instead to cruise off Newfoundland and attack British fishing boats.

Frantic pleas from Washington and Rochambeau changed the proud Admiral's mind. Reluctantly, Barras

New York City occupied only the southern tip of "York Island" in 1781, when English mapmakers drew the chart at right. Ships involved in British naval campaigns moved through channels of clearly marked depth and avoided the dangerous shoals (yellow).

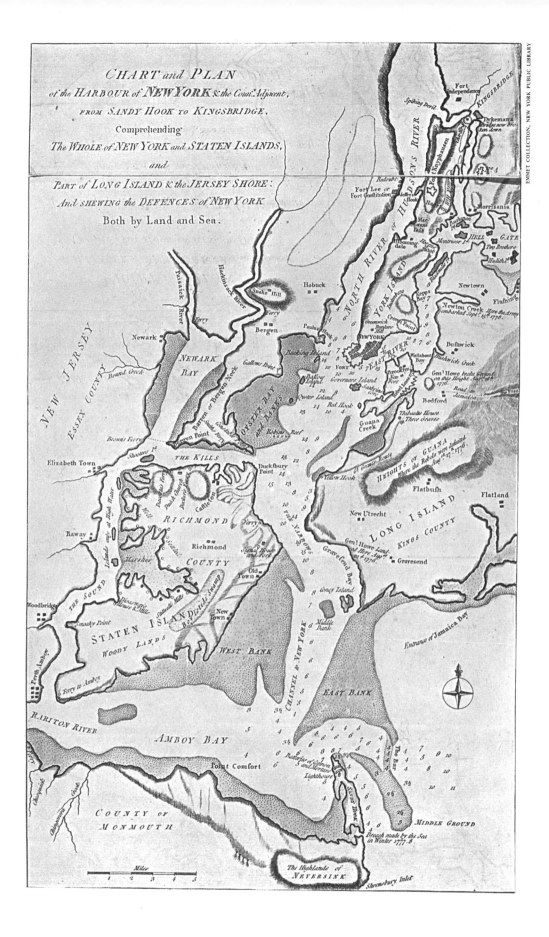

loaded the guns and beef and sailed for Virginia on August 23.

Now came the most important step of all—tricking Sir Henry Clinton into believing that the allies were still planning to attack New York. Fortunately, they had the unwitting assistance of some very efficient British spies. All through July, these well-paid secret agents had been telling Clinton that New York was Washington's goal. (And at the time, they were right.) As late as August 10, a British spy rode coolly through the entire allied camp at Dobbs Ferry and reported that the attack on New York was still definitely in the works.

Washington shrewdly encouraged this British presumption. Just before he began the march south, he met in his camp an "old inhabitant of New York" who was a known British spy. Washington blandly asked this gentleman what he knew about the water supply and the quality of the landing beaches on Long Island and terrain conditions around Sandy Hook. There was no special reason why he was asking, Washington explained. He was just "fond of knowing the Situation of different parts of the Country, as in the course of the war [I] might unexpectedly be called into that part of the Country." Then, as if just recalling he was a general, he gave the old Tory an alarmed look and urged him "by no means to lisp a Word of what had passed between [us]."

An even more elaborate deception was planned at about the same time.

So inadequate and untrustworthy were the official military communications networks that Washington often was forced to rely upon ordinary post riders to convey even the most confidential dispatches. Carried in boxes like the one above, such messages frequently were intercepted—giving the British advance notice of the allies' plans.

Washington issued orders to erect a large camp near Chatham, New Jersey, a town some twenty miles due east of Manhattan. A messenger carrying these orders deliberately passed so close to British lines that he was inevitably captured. Next, French bakers began constructing four huge ovens near Chatham, further "proof" that Washington had every intention of converting the site into a permanent camp from which he could launch his attack on New York.

On August 20 Washington detached two thirds of the allied army—2,500 of his own Americans and Rochambeau's 4,000 French troops—and crossed the Hudson River into New Jersey. He left behind 3,500

40

troops, under Major General William Heath, to hold the Hudson Valley. The Americans, practically destitute of supplies and equipment, crossed the river in a day. It took the French four days to get their elaborate supply train, their artillery, and their cavalry horses across. During this time, they anxiously looked over their shoulders to see what Clinton would do.

It was an unbelievably opportune moment for Sir Henry to strike. Even a feint could have thrown the allies into panic, and an aggressive commander might easily have destroyed the French as they struggled across the wide river, less than a day's march from the British forts in Manhattan. One French regimental commander, Lieutenant Colonel William de Deux-Ponts, noted in his journal: "An enemy a little bold and able would have seized the moment of our crossing the Hudson, so favorable for him, so embarrassing for us, for an attack. His indifference and lethargy at this moment is an enigma that cannot be solved by me."

Deux-Ponts, of course, had no idea how hard Washington had worked to bamboozle the British commander in chief. In New Jersey, the deception continued.

The allies carried with them across the Hudson some thirty large flatboats on wheels, further convincing the British that Washington intended to attack New York via Staten Island. But some more alert British officers were already beginning to doubt Washing-ton's intentions, even when he sent a decoy detachment tramping through the broiling August heat in the direction of Sandy Hook. On August 18 one lieutenant colonel informed Clinton that his spies reported depots of food and forage for the allied army all the way across New Jersey. But Clinton brushed off his warnings. On August 22 a New Jersey agent known as "Squib" wrote nervously to Clinton: "It is said they will go against New York, but some Circumstances, induce me to believe they will go to the Chesapeake. Yet for God's sake be prepared at all Points."

Benedict Arnold begged Clinton for six thousand men, guaranteeing that he would annihilate Washington and Rochambeau while their troops were strung out in a long exposed line of march in New Jersey. Clinton declined to risk a battle, and the disgusted Arnold told spymaster William Smith that he was now convinced that Clinton was prolonging the war for his personal gain.

On August 27 the allies were well into New Jersey when a messenger arrived with news that dismayed Washington and Rochambeau. General David Forman, who manned a coastal lookout near Sandy Hook, reported that "eighteen large ships of war" were entering New York harbor. Their colors were British.

Eighteen ships! It was the British West Indies squadron. For the first time Washington and Rochambeau realized that France was not the only

In a peep-show illustration even more fanciful than that of New York (page 24), German engravers envisioned Philadelphia as an American Venice, with stately palaces on a busy canal.

country capable of sending a fleet to the American coast. The British already had eleven ships in New York; if Forman's count of the arrivals was correct, there were twenty-nine British ships of the line ready to cruise off the Chesapeake. The combined fleet was more than enough to annihilate Barras' eight ships, which were sailing south with the vital salt beef provisions and siege cannon, and still give de Grasse a mauling that would make him abandon all thoughts of trapping Cornwallis.

Forman sent additional reports from Sandy Hook in the next few days. The British had only seven seaworthy ships of the line in New York, and the West Indies fleet actually had brought only thirteen additional vessels. The numbers were a little more comforting—twenty instead of twenty-nine—but the rest of the message was distinctly ominous. The entire British fleet had sailed from New York on August 31. The British chances of intercepting Barras at sea were still uncomfortably good.

Meanwhile, Washington had abandoned his efforts at deception in New Jersey and turned the heads of his columns toward the Delaware River. Not until September 2 did Clinton learn that the Americans and French were definitely headed south. On that very day Washington's men marched in blazing heat through Philadelphia, raising "a dust like a smothering snow."

Although half the city turned out to cheer them, Rochambeau and Washington found little to make them smile in Philadelphia. Since Robert Morris could not supply adequate water transportation, they had to abandon their plan of sending the troops south by ship. Artillery and heavy stores were committed to the few vessels Morris had been able to commandeer. As for money to pay the troops, Morris could proffer only the worthless Continental paper dollars.

A tense moment arose when the American troops made a direct request to the Continental Congress for at least a small advance on their back pay. Washington supported the request. Hurried conferences between Robert Morris and the congressmen resulted in a decision to borrow enough hard cash from the French army to give each of the men a few dollars. The next day Washington had the satisfaction of announcing that one month's pay in specie was to be distributed to all ranks except those who, "lost to all sense of honor, the pride of their profession and the love of their country, had deserted the Standard of Freedom at this critical moment."

Washington visited the Congress and could hardly have been cheered by what he saw there. The great names who had signed the Declaration of Independence were almost all gone. The weak Articles of Confederation had left the Congress without the power to tax or to command the separate states in almost any sphere. It could only recommend, and it had long since grown used to being ignored. By the summer of 1781, as many as five states did not even bother to send representatives; the morale of the members who did appear was low.

The French troops arrived in Philadelphia on the third and fourth of September. If the Americans caused excitement, the French were a sensation. One general, the Chevalier de Chastellux, later recalled the scene:

[The troops] made a halt about a mile from the city, and in an instant were dressed as elegantly as ever were the soldiers of a garrison on a day of royal review. They then marched through the town with military music playing, which is always particularly pleasing to the Americans. The streets were crowded with people, and the ladies appeared at the windows in their most splendid attire.

By the fifth of September, the entire allied army was on the road once more, the Americans in the first division and the slower-moving French behind them. The march now became a race to get to Virginia before the British could send reinforcements. They first had to get to the Chesapeake, where Washington felt certain there would be shipping to carry them on the last leg of their journey.

He already had written a number of his friends on Maryland's eastern shore to collect every available boat. Racing ahead of the army were other messengers urging the governors of Maryland and Delaware to accumulate supplies for the army en route and reminding them to rouse their militia. Still another messenger carried a letter to Lafayette, in which Washington urgently asked him for word of de Grasse and Barras.

From Philadelphia, Washington rode to Chester, Pennsylvania, but Comte Rochambeau went by water. When the little ship on which he made his journey pulled up to the Chester dock, Rochambeau and his staff were treated to a unique sight: George Washington was acting like a madman. He had his hat in one hand and his handkerchief in the other and was waving them both in wide, whooping circles. When the French General came down the gangplank, Washington threw his arms around him and shouted the glorious news: a messenger had just arrived from de Grasse's fleet. He was in the Chesapeake, with his twenty-nine ships and three thousand troops from the West Indies. The

Military duties kept Washington away from his estate for six years. This view of Mount Vernon, painted by an unknown artist in 1792, shows the frame mansion's east front.

soldiers were already ashore. Cornwallis was trapped!

Yet even this thrilling news did not mean that Washington's worries were over. His Maryland friends had been able to gather only enough ships to transport a third of the army down the Chesapeake. The rest had to be sent to Baltimore, to await transport

from de Grasse's fleet. Meanwhile, Washington, Rochambeau, and their staffs rode ahead and stopped for two days at Mount Vernon.

It was Washington's first return to his beloved plantation on the Potomac in six long years. After giving his guests a glimpse of Virginia hospitality at its most generous, Washington led them toward Williamsburg, where Lafayette was maintaining his watch on Cornwallis, fourteen miles away at Yorktown.

They were on the road little more than an hour on the morning of September 12 when a horseman came riding up to them with dismaying news: Admiral de Grasse had abandoned his blockade at the mouth of the Chesapeake. When the British fleet had appeared on the horizon, the French had gone to sea to battle them. Sounds of gunfire had been heard from shore, but both fleets had vanished into the vast Atlantic. No one knew whether France or Britannia ruled the waves.

TEXT CONTINUED ON PAGE 50

45

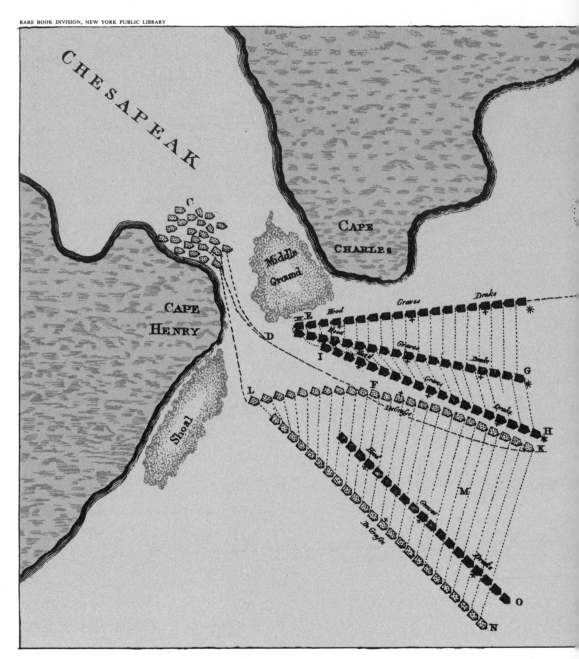

The most curious and perhaps the most crucial battle of the Revolution occurred on September 5, 1781. It was curious in that it involved the British and French, but no Americans, and in that it produced no victor while virtually ensuring Britain's ultimate defeat in the war. It was crucial in that it gave the Americans control over the Chesapeake, cutting Cornwallis off from aid or escape by sea, and giving the allies time to bring up their heavy siege guns.

In 1781 the British Admiral's nephew, William Graves, published the above chart in defense of his uncle's actions during the battle. The map reveals the unusual and inflexible pattern that such naval engagements invariably took, owing to the design of the ships and training of their captains. At 11 A.M. on the morning of the fifth, the British fleet (A), commanded by Graves and preceded by a lookout ship (B), approached the capes from the north, sighting de Grasse's

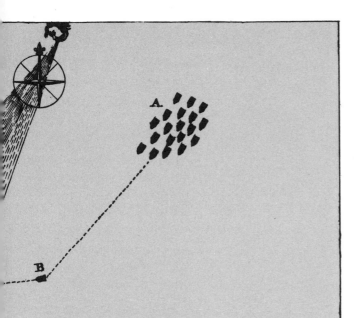

A: REPRESENTATION,

Of the Sea Fight, on the 5th of Sept 1781, between Rear Admiral **GRAVES** *and the Count* **DE GRASSE** *.*

French	24 Ships	1822 Guns	18.200 Men
English	19 Ships	1408 Guns	11.311 Men
The French Superior by 5 Ships		414 Guns	6889 Men

NB: Neither Fleet had at this time any land Forces aboard or in Transports.

Admiral Comte de Grasse

Admiral Thomas Lord Graves

French fleet (C) in the mouth of the bay. A sudden shift in the wind forced the British to "wear about" at the Middle Ground (E), which brought them into the traditional British windward attack position. As they did so, the French moved out to sea to engage them (D), and the two armadas met on nearly parallel courses. An error on Graves' part in judging the angle of approach forced the British van to engage the French singly, and they were unable to bring their fixed guns into position to return the enemy's broadsides. By sunset, both navies had drifted south (N, O), their disabled and dismasted ships unable to resume action. After another day of inconclusive feinting, the French turned north and disappeared. When the battered British fleet reached the mouth of the Chesapeake on the morning of September 13, the French blockade had been re-established, and Graves had to return with his fleet to New York.

De Grasse's tactical triumph over the British fleet in September, 1781, exactly reversed the results of an earlier battle. Following a similar contest on March 16, involving two other

6 MARCH 1781 ACTION OFF THE CHESAPEAKE

British and French fleets (above), it was the English who withdrew to guard the Chesapeake in the wake of an inconclusive engagement, and Lafayette who was cut off from reinforcement.

Messengers were immediately sent to the troopships coming down the Chesapeake, telling them to put ashore until further orders. It would be the end of everything if the allied army sailed into the guns of an English fleet. The two generals spent the night at Fredericksburg, Virginia, and pushed ahead the next morning at dawn. As usual, most of their party fell behind, unable to keep the pace Washington set. But another day ended without Williamsburg in sight, and it was not until the afternoon of September 14 that the small, dust-covered cavalcade rode through the streets of Williamsburg, past the handsome red brick "palace" where the royal governor had once lived.

At the camp of the French West Indian division, they were greeted by Lafayette, who liked to call himself Washington's adopted son. St. George Tucker, a young Bermudian who had moved to Virginia to join the Revolution, was standing only a few feet away and wrote his wife a vivid description of the scene. Lafayette "caught the General round his body, hugged him as close as it was possible, and absolutely kissed him from ear to ear once or twice . . ." This was, of course, a perfectly natural way for a Frenchman to express his deep affection, but it looked very strange to the Americans.

But the agonizing questions were: What news of de Grasse? Had Admiral Barras arrived? At dinner in the tent of the Marquis de Saint-Simon,

the French commander of the troops from the West Indies, there were only glum shakes of the head and worried, regretful *no*'s. Nevertheless, the French were determined to be gay. Saint-Simon's food was good, his wine was superb, and Lafayette filled Washington in on all that had been happening in Virginia while the latter was on the road south.

Cornwallis and his army had remained inert behind their fortifications at Yorktown. General Anthony Wayne had been wounded in the leg by a sentry when he failed to give the proper countersign while coming to visit Lafayette. The Marquis himself had spent two weeks in bed with malaria and in fact had staggered from his cot to his horse only to meet Washington.

Not until ten o'clock did the toasts and the serenades of the French army band end and let Washington retreat to his tent—and Lafayette to his sickbed to shake and shiver for another feverish night. Around twelve o'clock, before anyone could have been asleep, considering the anxiety de Grasse was causing them, an excited messenger came charging into camp with the wonderful news that the French fleet was back in the Chesapeake with a victory. The English fleet was so badly

The Marquis de Lafayette, twenty-four in 1781 and already a general, is the best known of many young Frenchmen who fought with and occasionally, like Lafayette, commanded Continental Army units.

damaged that it had retreated all the way to New York.

To everyone in the allied camp it seemed probable, even inevitable, that the British would return for another attempt to save Cornwallis. Washington and Rochambeau also knew that de Grasse had only a limited time to spend in American waters. They must attack Yorktown immediately. But their armies were still far up the Chesapeake.

Washington fired off a letter to Major General Benjamin Lincoln, who was shepherding the troops, urging all possible haste. "Every day we lose now is comparatively an age," he wrote. But he must have known that

Lincoln could not command the wind and tide. All that anyone could do for the time being was to worry and wait.

Their first communication from de Grasse did not lessen their anxiety. The moment Washington learned the good news of the naval victory, he wrote to the Admiral requesting the "honor of an interview" with him. He had no doubt learned something about de Grasse from Lafayette and probably had concluded already that the Admiral might be the weak link in the chain that they were drawing about Cornwallis. The moment he had arrived in the Chesapeake and put ashore Saint-Simon with his troops, de Grasse had wanted Lafayette to

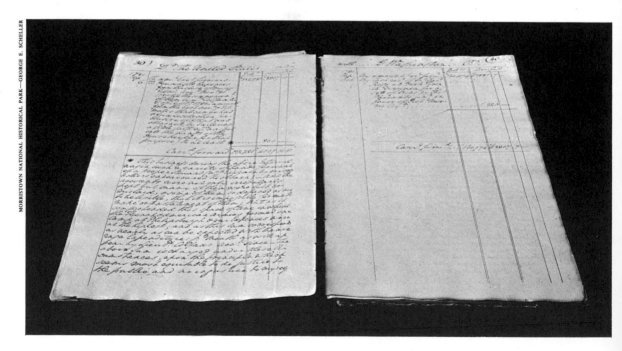

Washington's gravest problems in 1781 were not military, but financial. The nation was on the verge of bankruptcy and heavily in debt to its allies. Supplies and hard cash were scarce, and credit was nonexistent—as Yorktown entries in the General's ledger (above) attest.

launch an assault on the Yorktown entrenchments. The Marquis had wisely declined the opportunity, pointing out that their combined army was barely as strong as that of the English, who were dug in up to their chins.

De Grasse's answer to Washington's request, while it cordially welcomed the idea of a conference, ended with the same note of nervous impatience. "I am annoyed by the delay . . . time is passing, the enemy is profiting by it, and the season is approaching when against my will, I shall be obliged to forsake the allies for whom I have done my very best and more than could be expected."

De Grasse was by no means the only worry. Supplies, that perpetual problem, were alarmingly low. Four days before, Lafayette, in the midst of his malaria attack, had written frantically to Virginia's new governor, Thomas Nelson: "I could wish to sleep tonight but I fear it will be impossible with the prospect that is before us tomorrow. There is not one grain of flour in camp whether for the American or French army."

The nine thousand men already in the allied camp were living from day to day on a trickle of food from the surrounding countryside. Yet the harvest in both Virginia and Maryland had been exceptionally rich; it was a question of organizing the transportation and spending freely the 800,000 gold piastres that de Grasse had borrowed in Havana, Cuba. The two generals handed the money to Claude Blanchard, the French commissary, and told him to get busy.

The commissary was appalled. He was the very model of the government worker—fussy, precise, proud of order, and in love with organization. But his staff, his supplies, his secretary—everything he needed in order to function properly—were still on the Chesapeake with the rest of the army. "I set to work," he wrote, "though without a piece of paper or an employee or a bag of flour at my disposal; I was completely overwhelmed." Lafayette, used to dealing with the Virginians, volunteered to help and won Blanchard's heart completely. (The commissary found fault with almost everyone else, including Rochambeau, whose manners he pronounced far from courteous.) Blanchard ordered ovens to be built, "but I was in want of tools and had to run about much and negotiate to obtain even a hammer." The climax to his woes was a nocturnal catastrophe; the house in which he had stored the 800,000 gold piastres was old and weak; in the middle of the night Blanchard was frightened from his bed on the second floor by a tremendous crash. He rushed downstairs to find his servant in the cellar, up to his neck in gold coins. The whole first floor had given way under the weight of the hard cash.

Meanwhile, Washington had given warm approval to Baron Friedrich von Steuben's suggestion that he improve the polish of the American army with

A PLAN of
YORK TOWN AND GLOUCESTER,
IN THE PROVINCE OF VIRGINIA,
Shewing
the WORKS constructed for the Defence of those Posts
by the BRITISH ARMY,
under the Command of Lt. Genl. EARL CORNWALLIS;
together with
the Attacks and Operations of the American and French Forces,
Commanded by
GENl. WASHINGTON and COUNT ROCHAMBEAU,
to whom the said Posts were Surrendered
on the 17th October 1781.
from an actual SURVEY in the Possession of
Jno. HILLS, late Lieut. in the 23d Regt. & Asst. Engr.
YORK RIVER
GLOUCESTER
GLOUCESTER POINT
1000 Yards
YORK TOWN
SUNKEN VESSELS
SECOND
FIRST
PARALLEL
French Batteries
American Battery

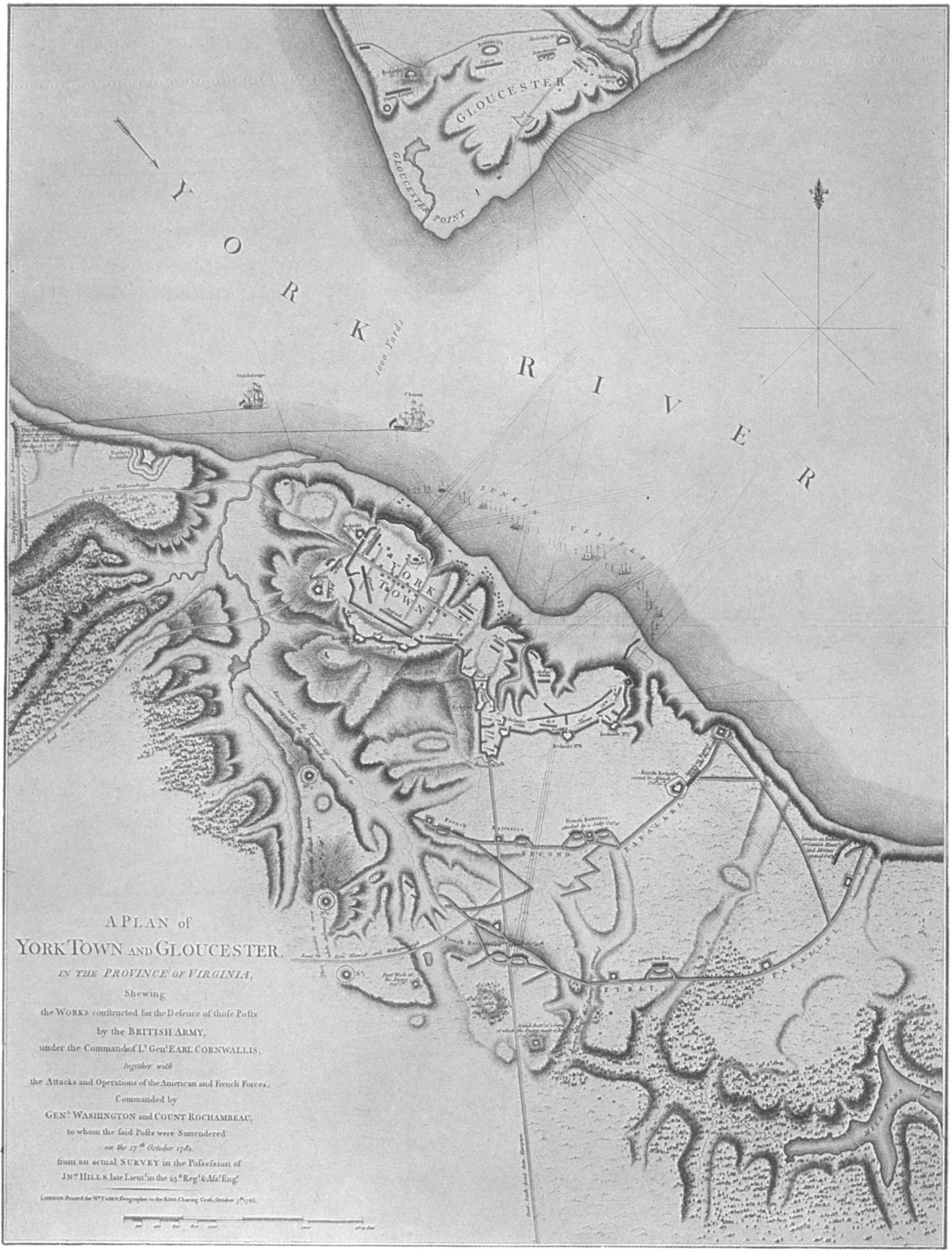

a little drilling. Both the Baron and Lafayette were determined to show the French that their American "sans culottes" (Von Steuben had coined the phrase at Valley Forge—it means "without breeches") could be as professional as the gaudiest of the French grenadiers.

Almost certainly, the Baron was in the same rare form that had endeared him to Americans since Valley Forge. The slightest mistake on the drill field caused him to explode. In spite of his thunderings, there were few generals in the army to whom the men were more devoted. The Baron was always bankrupt, because he could not stop handing out his money to soldiers in distress. He spent as much again on feeding his junior officers at his famous suppers. "Poor fellows," he would say, "they have field officers' stomachs without their pay or rations."

While the Baron drilled, Washington showed his gift for personal leadership. The day after he arrived, he held a reception before his tent for all the officers in the American camp. Lieutenant Ebenezer Denny of Pennsylvania noted in his diary: "Officers all pay their respects to the Commander in Chief. Go in a body. Those who are not personally known, their names given by General Hand and General Wayne. He stands in the door, takes every man by the hand. The officers all pass in, receiving his salute and shake. . . ."

On September 17 Washington and Rochambeau met Admiral de Grasse aboard his huge, three-deck flagship, the *Ville de Paris*. They came away in a most uneasy frame of mind. The hearty, six-foot-two-inch-tall Admiral was cordial and frank in his replies to Washington's questions. He was ready to lend them some of his marines, but none of his powder, which he might need if the English fleet returned. But he horrified Washington and Rochambeau by first saying that he could not stay past October 15. He then admitted that extreme necessity could persuade him to delay his departure until the end of the month, but not a day longer. He already had risked too much for his own good, de Grasse explained. Originally, his orders were to take only twelve ships to America and use the rest of his fleet to escort a valuable convoy home from the French West Indies. He had canceled the sailing date of the convoy and brought with him every available ship. He had to be back in the West Indies by mid-November, not only to get the convoy on its way, but also to keep a pledged date with the Spanish, who needed his ships for a joint operation against British Jamaica.

Cornwallis insisted that his position was "bad," but Yorktown was actually far from indefensible. Flanked by Yorktown Creek (left) and the mill pond feeding Wormley Creek (right), and protected on the York River side by high cliffs, the city was vulnerable from but one direction (center).

The two troubled generals returned to Williamsburg. Their only consolation during a stormy voyage back across the Chesapeake was the sight of French and American transports arriving from Maryland with the bulk of their troops. They sent them orders to land immediately.

It had been a wearisome voyage. Some men had spent fourteen days in open boats on the choppy autumn waters of the great bay, constantly on the lookout for British cruisers. Their troubles did not end with their landing at Williamsburg.

Joseph Plumb Martin, a sergeant in the sappers and miners (today we call them engineers), said that his regiment had nothing to eat when they went into camp—not an unusual predicament for a Continental soldier. Martin and another sergeant "concluded to go after the provisions, to stretch our legs after so long confinement on board the vessel." With them went the company cook, "for he as usual had nothing to do at home."

Arriving at the camp commissary, Martin and his two companions found men from dozens of other units already in line; it would obviously be hours before they were served. Reluctantly, with some of the precious hard money they had received at Philadelphia, they purchased a side of beef from neighborhood butchers. (The cash, Martin said, was "the first that could be called money which we had received as wages since the year '76 or that we ever did receive till the close

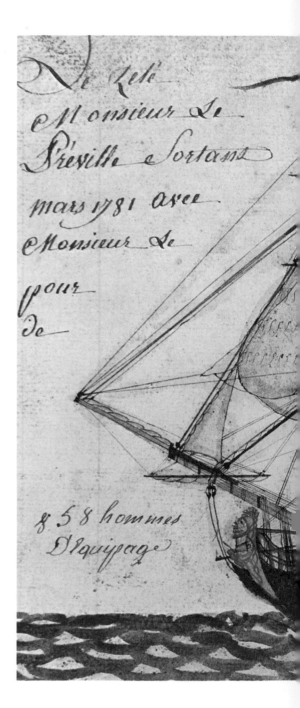

Commandez Par
Chevallier de Grasse
de Brest Le 20
L'Escadre De
Comte De Grass
Les Jlles
Lamerique

The ill-fated Zélé was one of twenty-four ships under de Grasse's command during his naval duel with Graves off Chesapeake Bay. Like the others, this seventy-four-gun frigate was sluggish under sail but capable of awesome broadside fire. Moored with the fleet in the West Indies, six months after the Yorktown victory, the Zélé parted her cables and drifted off. Pursuing her, de Grasse encountered Rodney's superior British fleet and was defeated.

57

of the war, or indeed ever after.") They hoisted the beef on their cook's back and sent him off to camp, so that he could have it ready for them when they returned. It was a fatal mistake.

The cook [Martin said], who had been a bank fisherman and of course loved to wet his whistle once in a while, set off for home and we contented ourselves till after dark before we could get away. . . . When we came home we went directly to our tent to get our suppers, when, lo, we found Mr. Cook fast asleep in the tent and not the least sign of cookery going on. With much ado we waked him and inquired where our victuals were. He had not none, he mumbled out as well as he could.

"Where is the pluck you brought home?"

"I sold it," said he.

"Sold it! What did you sell it for?"

"I don't know," was the reply.

"If you have sold it, what did you get for it?"

"I will tell you," said he. "First I got a little rum, and next I got a little pepper and—and—then I got a little more rum."

"Well, and where is the rum and pepper you got?"

"I drank the rum," said he, "there is the pepper."

"Pox on you," said the sergeant. "I'll pepper you."

The second sergeant started to thrash the cook, but Sergeant Martin intervened in his favor. "But truly," he admitted later, "I was hungry and impatient enough to have eaten the fellow had he been well cooked and peppered."

Hungry or full, Martin and his comrades in arms were in the ranks at

A 1784 German water color depicts a rather immaculate American sharpshooter (left) and a member of the Pennsylvania infantry.

5 A.M. on September 28 when Washington ordered the allied army down the road from Williamsburg to Yorktown. With over three thousand militia from Maryland and Virginia, and the French reinforcements from the West Indies, he now commanded 18,993 men. The American light infantry were the advance guard, moving with field artillery interspersed among their companies so that they could be ready to give battle the instant they encountered opposition. In his orders, Washington told the soldiers to use the bayonet if they were attacked; he expected them to disprove the British boast that they were the only ones to decide battles with that weapon. Finally the General sug-

gested that the two nations compete for honor, yet co-operate for victory.

Sergeant Martin did not see the march in such lofty terms, but his thoughts were equally forceful:

We prepared to move down and pay our old acquaintance, the British, at Yorktown, a visit. I doubt not but their wish was not to have so many of us come at once as their accommodations were rather scanty. They thought, "the fewer the better cheer." We thought, "the more the merrier." We had come a long way to see them and were unwilling to be put off with excuses.

The British did not make the slightest attempt to harass the allied advance down the long, thickly wooded peninsula. Not until the first light infantrymen reached the end of the woods, and fanned out along the shores of Yorktown and Wormley creeks—two small streams that formed natural barriers on the right and left flanks of the British position—did the first British gun speak.

Cannons and muskets boomed and barked from behind little forts, known as redoubts, across both these creeks and in the center, where the main road ran. The Americans and French returned the fire. But they were more interested in peeking through the trees, past these outlying British fortifications, at the prize beyond them.

In the late September sunshine they could see the roofs of Yorktown's red brick houses about a half mile away, surrounded by a jagged semicircle of inner fortifications, the red,

The natty uniform at left was prescribed for members of Washington's cavalry; at right, for the commander in chief himself.

white, and blue Union Jack flying defiantly over them. Peering through their telescopes, the American and French commanders counted ten formidable redoubts, with over sixty "embrasures"—openings through which cannon fired. On the ramparts of each redoubt stood solid columns of sharply pointed stakes, known as palisades. Before them were deep ditches and "abatis"—thick, sharpened tree trunks, angled from the ground to impale a would-be attacker. Could they fight their way through these outer forts, and crack that bristling network of inner forts, before Admiral de Grasse's deadline expired? That was the question Washington and Rochambeau could not answer.

4

CLOSING IN ON CORNWALLIS

Inside Yorktown, at this point, an air of sturdy optimism prevailed among officers and men. Sir Henry Clinton had assured Cornwallis that he was coming to help him, with at least four thousand men, the "instant" Admiral Graves said that the battered British fleet was ready to sail again. Convinced of England's supremacy on the seas, Cornwallis was certain that the revived fleet would clear the way for this reinforcement by decisively defeating de Grasse.

Cornwallis also assured his officers and men that the allies were weak in artillery. He did not see how they could possibly have transported anything heavier than field artillery, whose shot would bounce off his redoubts like tennis balls. It apparently never even occurred to the British commander that Admiral Barras would bring the French siege guns from Newport. Britain, after all, com-

Heavily damaged during the siege (when it served as Cornwallis' headquarters), Yorktown's Nelson house was privately restored early in this century. An eighteenth-century sundial now graces the formal gardens.

61

manded the sea lanes between New York and Virginia.

Many of Cornwallis' men were looking forward to a battle. Samuel Graham, the twenty-five-year-old captain of a regiment that was composed of unruly Scottish Highlanders, told of seeing "an old Highland gentleman, a lieutenant," standing one evening on one of the outer redoubts. Flashing his sword, the man was saying: "Come on, Maister Washington, I'm unco glad to see you; I've been offered money for my commission, but I could na think of gangin hame without a sight of you. Come on."

Equally tough and spoiling for a fight were the Royal Welsh Fusiliers, one of the most famous regiments in the British army. Some of its men had died at Bunker Hill, and the unit had been in almost every major battle of the past six years. On the march through the Carolinas, the Fusiliers had lost 210 of their 360 men, but Cornwallis showed his confidence in the battered regiment by putting it in charge of the strategic star-shaped redoubt that guarded the right flank of his inner lines.

Not so enthusiastic were three other regiments in Cornwallis' army. Two were from a little principality on the Rhine known as Anspach-Bayreuth. A third regiment came from the nearby duchy of Hesse-Cassel. Their soldiers spoke German, and they had been "sold" to the British by their royal masters. The British paid an average of 7 pounds, 4 shillings, 4½ pence for each of these soldiers, plus "blood money" of 30 crowns for every man killed and roughly a third of that sum for every man who lost an arm or leg.

More deeply committed to the defense of Yorktown were some 840 men of the Royal Navy. There were twenty-four transports, two frigates, and numerous other smaller craft in the York River harbor. Notable among these sailors was a pop-eyed, excitable young man named Bartholomew James. Only twenty-nine years old, he had been fighting in America and the West Indies since 1776. He had been captured by the French in 1778 and had spent a year of harrowing imprisonment on the island of Santo Domingo. James was serving as a lieutenant aboard the frigate *Charon*, but when the French fleet appeared, he was ordered to take command of a captured American sloop. He thus began a dangerous game of cat and mouse with de Grasse.

On September 1 James was asked to guard an express boat with dispatches for New York. At midnight his sloop escorted the boat past the French ships blockading the York River's mouth, then past the rest of the enemy fleet at the entrance to Chesapeake Bay. Before dawn he was back at York. His cockleshell with a crew of thirty had passed undetected under the very noses of the 19,000 sailors of de Grasse's armada.

A week later, James was sent down the river to "reconnoiter the enemy's

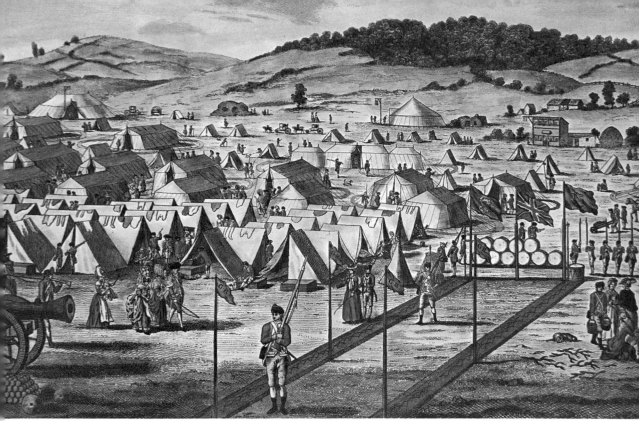

The informality evident in this 1780 view of a British encampment—with ladies paying call and laundry hung on ridgepoles—belies the strict regimen that characterized English camps.

fleet" when it sailed off to fight Admiral Graves. For two days and two nights, James prowled about the bay, reporting de Grasse's return from the sea battle and counting the enemy fleet, with the addition of Barras' ships, as "thirty-six sail of the line, besides frigates, fireships, bombs and transports."

On the morning of September 11, Lieutenant James was horrified to see the entire French armada weigh anchor and start straight for him while he lay totally becalmed. De Grasse was only shifting his position, however; he had no interest in a fleet attack of James' piddling sloop. But the leading French frigate, more than willing to pounce on him, made directly for James from a distance of about three miles. "By bringing with them a sea breeze," James wrote, "they came very near me before I could get any wind; at six o'clock one of the headmost ships fired a shot at me, at which time, having received the wind, I cut away my boat and hopped off, with all I could drag on her, and fortunately escaped '*Monsieur.*'"

This was not the end of Lieutenant James' adventures. Two French frigates and a ship of the line were blockading the mouth of the York River. If these sentinels could be destroyed by fire ships, de Grasse might withdraw all his ships out into the Chesapeake. With the river mouth open, Cornwallis could embark his forces in small boats some dark night and make for the southern side of the bay, where he could leg it for the Carolinas.

There was only one established fire ship—appropriately named the *Vulcan*—among the British ships tied up at York. But four schooners were quickly converted—a process requiring nothing more than a plentiful supply of tarred faggots and sailors with good nerves. Lieutenant James volunteered for command of one fire ship; lieutenants Conway and Symonds, also of the Royal Navy, asked for and received two others. The fourth was assigned to Mr. Campbell, the American-born captain of a loyalist privateer, on whom the British looked with considerable suspicion.

On September 22 (the day Washington returned from his conference with de Grasse aboard the *Ville de*

As this 1775 cartoon suggests, a British soldier's life was one of extreme hardship. Nonetheless, the ill-paid redcoat (surrounded here by his equally gaunt and ragged family) was better off than his American counterpart, who often received no uniform and fought without pay.

Paris), the wind was between the north and west—just right for a fire ship assault. Lieutenant James described the scene:

We cut our cables at midnight, and ran down the river. At two o'clock we came within sight of the enemy, and were advancing with every probability of success when from some cause, unaccountable as strange, Mr. Campbell of the privateer set fire to his vessel. This proved as unfortunate as dangerous, for the enemy, who was before keeping no lookout, cut their cables, beat to quarters, and having fired twenty or thirty shot at us, retreated in a precipitate and confused manner.

Lieutenants Conway and Symonds promptly set fire to their vessels. With the whole river aglow, James could now see French launches rowing toward him. There was no quarter asked or given to sailors aboard fire ships, and so James "set fire to my vessel, with no other view than to prevent her falling into the hands of the enemy," and took to his boat.

Only the captain of the regular fire ship, *Vulcan*, maintained his nerve, waiting until the last possible moment to ignite his vessel. From his rowboat, James watched the *Vulcan* blaze up "within her own length" of the bow of a French seventy-four-gun ship of the line. But the French ship avoided her, and when the *Vulcan* bore down on another vessel, she received a broadside from the French and veered off to consume herself in the dark waters of the bay.

The disgruntled James never knew that the French, far from "keeping no lookout," were waiting for the five British fire ships all the time. The captain of a captured British schooner had revealed that the attack was scheduled for midnight.

After the failure of the fire ships, the British could only brace themselves for the American assault. Washington's men appeared through the trees on September 28, and for a day and a half the two armies feinted and sparred while the Americans reconnoitered the British fortifications. The French made an exploratory attack on the star-shaped redoubt that commanded the British right flank. The Royal Welsh Fusiliers met them with furious cannon fire and musketry, and the French fell back, with one man dead and two wounded.

The skirmishing continued throughout the next day. The British and German soldiers manning the outer lines were sure that at any moment they would be fighting for their lives. It seemed obvious that Washington would have to storm their positions if he hoped to begin the more serious work of cracking the inner lines. If they fought well, they could cost Washington so many men that he might think twice about repeating the performance against the far more formidable inner redoubts.

At midnight on September 29, Cornwallis sent his men in the outer lines a startling order: Retreat. Reluctantly, the soldiers abandoned the trenches and redoubts that they had sweated to build and silently stole

back across the open meadow to the inner fortifications circling Yorktown. The diary of one German soldier, Stephan Popp, leaves little doubt of the impact on the men's morale. "The regiments in the line moved back to the city because the enemy always came nearer and stronger. . . . In the night three of the men of our company deserted."

What happened? What was going on in Cornwallis' mind? The explanation was not to be found in the British command at Yorktown but in headquarters at New York. Sir Henry Clinton had sent Cornwallis another reassuring letter, telling him that in "a few days" he would board the fleet with five thousand men to "relieve you and afterwards cooperate with you."

This was Cornwallis' reason for retiring to his inner lines. If he waited for the allies to advance, some of his forward redoubts might have been cut off by a successful attack. The army left to defend the inner line would have been that much smaller. Retreating gave him the best chance of retaining a compact striking force until Sir Henry arrived with his reinforcements.

Undoubtedly Cornwallis knew that a retreat would dampen the morale of

The astounded allies awoke on September 30 to find the outer British redoubts (at left center, between Wormley and Yorktown creeks) deserted. Expecting reinforcements momentarily, the British had withdrawn during the night to Yorktown's more easily defended inner fortifications. The English were far from beaten, however; led by Scammell (right), the first Americans to venture into the abandoned area were ambushed and Scammell was fatally wounded.

his men. But there were times, he reasoned, when tactics were more important than morale. That night the General sat down at his desk in the Nelson mansion and told his commander in chief that he had "ventured these last two days to look General Washington's whole force in the face" from the outer works and "there was but one wish throughout the whole army, which was, that the enemy would advance." The army would now retire to the inner forts, he said, and if Clinton arrived "in any reasonable time," he would find York and Gloucester "in possession of his Majesty's troops."

Early the next morning, September 30, Colonel Alexander Scammell, the officer of the day for the American wing of the allied army, made the astonishing discovery that the British had abandoned their outer redoubts.

At first the French and Americans could not believe their good fortune. Not until noon did they send detachments into the works.

Washington wrote excitedly to the President of the Congress that the British move had handed the allies "very advantageous Grounds." The French Colonel William de Deux-Ponts inspected the abandoned works with Rochambeau and noted in his journal that the allies were now "masters of all the approaches to the place."

In the afternoon of the same day, the Americans learned that the British were by no means ready to surrender. Colonel Scammell rode out with a few other officers to reconnoiter the enemy inner lines. He could not have been more than a few hundred yards away from the men in the captured

67

Admired for his bravura and feared for his ruthlessness, cavalry leader Banastre Tarleton was every bit as dashing as he appears in this 1782 engraving of Sir Joshua Reynolds' painting.

outer fortifications when—before any-one could seize a musket or shout a warning—out of a clump of woods whirled a squadron of British dragoons. Sabers drawn, they instantly cut Scammell's party off from the American lines. Resistance would have been suicidal. Scammell and his mortified men could only surrender.

While some dragoons were seizing the reins of Scammell's horse, one of the British officers charged up, pistol in hand, and shot him in the back. It was an act of senseless brutality, which Cornwallis obviously regretted when he learned of it. He had British surgeons dress Scammell's wound, and under a flag of truce, had an officer conduct him into the allied lines as a paroled prisoner. The American doctors who examined the wound shook their heads mournfully. It was fatal. Scammell died a few days later.

Washington had to maintain a simultaneous siege on the British post at Gloucester across the York River, to make sure that Cornwallis did not attempt to break out in that direction. There an uneasy alliance prevailed between the American General George Weedon, commanding mostly militia volunteers, and the Duc de Lauzun, the elegant nobleman whose "legion" of cavalry comprised the only horse soldiers at Washington's disposal. Opposing him was the British cavalryman Colonel Banastre Tarleton.

Both cavalry commanders were itching for a chance to meet in head-on combat, and they got it on the morn-ing of October 3. Lauzun was leading his legion down a lane toward Gloucester Point, as part of a move to tighten the American lines around the British camp. About four miles from the British position they discovered a wagon train and several dozen cattle. It was a British foraging party guarded by Tarleton and his dragoons. Lauzun knew how badly the British needed the food. He ordered a charge, and soon both sides of the little lane were crowded with cursing, sweating, saber-swinging horsemen.

The rival commanders swiftly spotted each other, and Tarleton, fearless as always, tried to cut his way through to Lauzun. Just as they were about to meet, one of Lauzun's legionnaires speared the horse of a nearby British trooper. The dying animal toppled under Tarleton's steed, and the young Colonel crashed to the ground in a wild tangle of men and horseflesh.

The French shouted exultantly. They thought that they had Tarleton captured and his men routed. But Tarleton's troopers were tough professional soldiers. With angry loyalty, they surrounded their fallen Colonel and defended him ferociously until an aide brought another horse. To give his men a chance to regroup, Tarleton ordered them to file behind the light infantry company of the Royal Welsh Fusiliers, who had by now arrived to form a line of battle.

Recklessly disregarding the principle that cavalry should not attack well-positioned infantry, Lauzun charged. A volley from the British foot soldiers emptied a dozen of his saddles, and his shaken troops fled for cover. Fortunately for the French, a battalion of Virginia militia under Lieutenant Colonel John Francis Mercer arrived as the horsemen reeled back, and Lauzun wisely retreated behind them to regroup.

Tarleton had no respect for American militia. He ordered a charge, hoping to catch Lauzun and his horsemen before they reformed. But the British leader abruptly discovered that these Virginians were no ordinary militiamen. Most, including Mercer, were veterans of the Continental Line who had long fought under Washington. Instead of scattering in panic, they met the British charge with a blast of fire that sent Tarleton's horsemen scampering back to their infantry once more. The Royal Welsh Fusiliers advanced to support Tarleton, and Mercer's men met them with a volley that killed their lieutenant and wounded several other soldiers.

By this time, the foraging party was safely inside the British lines. Tarleton decided that it was foolish to waste more men on such skirmishing. Slowly he pulled back, deliberately keeping his forces in a compact body. Lauzun also decided to waste no more men and did not charge again.

Washington was delighted by news of the action. He complimented his fellow Virginians for their bravery and also was careful to congratulate the Duc de Lauzun for the "decisive

vigour with which he charged the enemy." The commander in chief called the affair a "brilliant success."

Washington obviously felt that his men could use this boost to their morale, because on the Yorktown side they were doing more digging than fighting. All during the first week of October the soldiers, both French and American, hefted shovels and swung picks to convert the captured British forts into a siege line.

The British retaliated with a constant and often deadly bombardment. One day a single cannon ball killed four men in the Pennsylvania Line. On October 2 a Pennsylvania colonel, Richard Butler, counted 352 enemy rounds. Another American tells of a militiaman who threw away his shovel and did a mocking dance on the wall of his parapet for the better part of an hour, while cannon balls hissed around him. Why his officers allowed him to continue this idiocy is a mystery. The story has a sad ending. A cannon ball finally "put an end to his capers."

General George Washington did not indulge in sideshow antics, but during his frequent trips along the front lines to reconnoiter the enemy fortification, he often exposed himself almost as recklessly to the British gunners. On the first of October a worried aide ordered a guard of fifty men from the Pennsylvania Line to cover Washington, lest the British try to take him prisoner. The commander in chief, along with the French engineer Duportail and three men of the guard, advanced to within three hundred yards of the enemy's main works. This was outside the rifle range of two hundred yards, and Washington therefore was probably safe from British sharpshooters. Yet, Colonel Philip Van Cortlandt of New York reported that one cannon ball came so close that most of the aides and guards hastily retreated. Washington did not even lower his field glasses.

Another day, a cannon ball showered pebbles and dirt over Washington's whole party. Chaplain Evans of the light infantry was so alarmed that he pointed out to the general the debris on his hat before brushing it off. "Mr. Evans," Washington said with a smile, "you had better carry that home and show it to your wife and children."

More than a few of Washington's soldiers were itching to return some of the shot the British had been blasting at them. But there were no cannon in position on the allied side of the lines. The American artillery commander, Major General Henry Knox, and his men had searched half of Tidewater Virginia for wagons and horses to drag the heavy guns and ammunition over the sandy road from nearby Trebell's Landing, where the French ships had unloaded them. Washington volunteered his own baggage wagons and asked all the general officers to follow his example. Other officers contributed horses, but the army simply did not have enough animals. Many of the metal monsters had to be dragged by enlisted men.

Not until the fourth of October did any artillery reach the vicinity of the front lines. Such slow progress must have been agonizing to Washington. His original schedule had called for opening a new parallel, as siege lines were called, by October 1.

Elsewhere back of the lines, the hospitals were not yet ready for the sick and wounded. The French commissary, Claude Blanchard, was in a state of near panic because all the

Etched on a Revolutionary powder horn, this unique sketch shows Continental soldiers (in remarkably accurate uniforms) moving a limbered American siege cannon toward enemy lines.

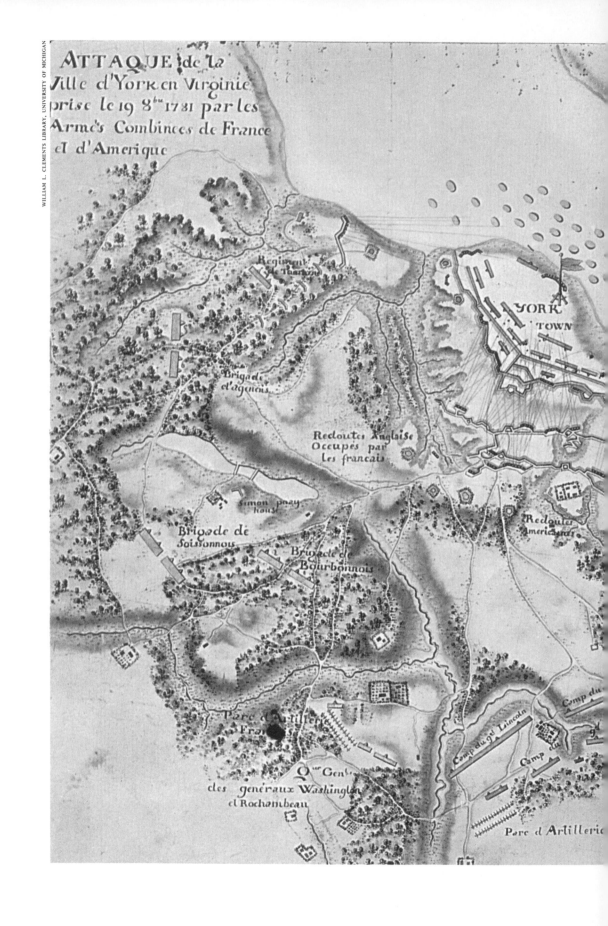

ATTAQUE de la
Ville d'York en Virginie
prise le 19 8bre 1781 par les
Armées Combinées de France
et d'Amerique

Regiment
de Touraine

Brigade
d'agenois

Redoutes Anglaise
Occupés par
les francais

YORK
TOWN

Simon poay
house

Brigade de
Soissonnois

Brigade de
Bourbonnois

Redoutes
Americaines

Parc d'Artillerie
Fran.

Qer Genl
des généraux Washington
et Rochambeau

Camp du gal Lincoln

Camp du

Camp

Camp du

Parc d'Artillerie

medicines and other equipment for his hospital were still on ships in the James River. By September 28, the harried commissary was fretting over three hundred sick enlisted men and ten officers. The ten officers "were harder to please than all the rest."

While all these various departments of the twenty-thousand-man allied army were bracing for the moment of contact with the enemy, Washington kept in close touch with other theatres of war. He corresponded regularly with Major General William Heath, on the Hudson, who sent south all he could learn about British plans in New York. Washington was even more anxious about Nathanael Greene, who, in spite of a perpetual shortage of men and guns, was still fighting a separate war in South Carolina.

Finally, on the morning of October 6, Henry Knox reported to Washington that the backbreaking job of moving the siege artillery and ammunition into the front lines was done. It was the best news that the commander in chief had heard in a weary week. That afternoon he wrote to the President of the Congress: "We shall this night open trenches."

While Cornwallis' men dug in behind the city's walls (top), the Americans and the French moved cautiously forward in preparation for the siege itself. Washington's headquarters, as well as those of Lincoln and Rochambeau, can be seen at the bottom of this highly detailed 1781 French map.

5

"OPEN TRENCHES"

Sergeant Joseph Plumb Martin tells in his memoirs what the words "open trenches" meant to the men of the Continental Army. He and the other members of the sappers and miners moved into the rainy darkness on the night of October 6. Under the direction of French engineering officers, they began digging into the sandy earth about eight hundred yards from the British redoubts. Twenty-five hundred other Americans, with loaded muskets, crouched only a few yards away, ready to give these unarmed toilers their instant support.

Suddenly the French officers ordered them to stop. Warning them not to straggle a foot either to left or to right, they disappeared into the gloom. The men grew jittery, so close to British muskets and cannon without a scrap of cover. "We now began to be a little jealous of our safety," Martin said later, "being without arms and within forty rods of the British trenches."

It was really 160 rods, but the darkness made the British seem much closer to the uneasy Martin and his

friends. Their worries doubled when out of the darkness appeared a man wearing what seemed to be an overcoat. A civilian.

What was the stranger doing there? Was he a daring loyalist spy, trying to find out how many men Cornwallis should order to the attack? The Americans became even more alarmed when the mysterious visitor asked them the names of their regiments and where the French engineers had gone. They mumbled vague replies and almost sneered when he advised them to say nothing to the enemy if taken prisoner. "We were obliged to him for his kind advice," said Martin, "but we considered ourselves as standing in no great need of it. For we knew as well as he did that sappers and miners were allowed no quarter by the laws of warfare."

Saying that he would find the French engineering officers, the man in the overcoat vanished. The sappers waited, muttering curses on their allies and on the rain, which now was coming down in a steady drizzle. A few minutes later, the familiar figures

Allied soldiers digging the first parallel, or network of trenches, worked at night—when the danger of being spotted by British marksmen occupying the forward redoubts was reduced. One such redoubt (above), preserved as part of a national park, still flies the Union Jack.

75

of the French engineers loomed out of the night. The stranger was with them. Martin, standing close by, did some eavesdropping. He caught his breath when he heard one officer say: "Your Excellency . . ." It could mean only one thing.

The "civilian" was General George Washington.

"Had we dared," Martin said, "we would have cautioned him for exposing himself so carelessly to danger at such a time—and doubtless he would have taken it in good part if we had . . ."

Sergeant Martin and his friends may have griped about the drizzle in which they worked. But George Washington probably said a silent prayer of thanksgiving for the cloudy sky. If the night of October 6 had been clear, there would have been a half moon illuminating Yorktown, making the men easy targets for the British artillery.

The "great trench" that they were digging was to start at the head of Yorktown Creek, near the center of the peninsula, and swing in a long arc to the high bank of the York River, where it would come about six hundred yards from the two forward British redoubts.

To confuse the enemy artillery, Washington ordered fires built beyond a marsh on the far right of the British works and had several dozen men tramp back and forth in front of of them. Deceived into thinking that a large body of infantry was massing, the befuddled British gunners fired at these decoys. Their shots whistled harmlessly over the heads of the Americans, who were entrenching, as Martin said, somewhat inaccurately, "literally under their noses."

The trench was a big job for a single night's work. One officer said that it was 3,840 to 4,480 feet long, and there were also four redoubts to be constructed, two supporting each flank. For the redoubts, the men had to lug forward tons of fascines and gabions. A fascine was a long bundle of brushwood tied tightly together, and a gabion was a wicker basket, shaped like a cylinder, filled with dirt. Together they formed the base for the dirt walls the men threw up around them. The diggers needed little urging to make the dirt fly; they knew what would happen if the dawn found them unprotected. "The men employed that night eat no 'idle bread' (and I question if they eat any other)," Joseph Plumb Martin said. When the sun rose, the Americans were working securely behind a solid barricade. They had not lost a single man in the entire night's cannonade.

At dawn, the British guns began blasting away more accurately, but the digging men were so well protected that they could regard the barrage as more amusing than dangerous. A British bulldog added to the sport by chasing the cannon balls when they bounded off the thick American walls. "Our officers wished to catch him and oblige him to carry a message from them into the town to his masters, but he looked too formidable for any of us to encounter," Sergeant Martin said.

By noon the trenches were ready for the formal opening of the siege. Lafayette's division was given the honor of occupying them first, and the light infantry regiment commanded by Lieutenant Colonel Alexander

Promoted rapidly during his six-year war service, Alexander Hamilton was less than twenty-six when he served as Washington's aide-de-camp during the Yorktown siege.

Hamilton led the way. With proud precision he obeyed article twenty-five of Washington's siege regulations, which were based on centuries-old military traditions: "All the troops either relieving or relieved will March with Drums beating, Colors flying." Regulation twenty-six stipulated that the "standard bearers will plant their standards" on the very top of the trench wall.

Captain James Duncan of Hamilton's regiment looked forward to this formality with some uneasiness. He was the man who would have to do the planting, an act that would make him a perfect target for the British gunners. He also feared that the regiment would be decimated while it marched to the trench, beating its drums and flaunting its flags. But the French engineers knew their business. They had laid out the trenches so that ravines on either side served as "covered ways"—the traditional method of approaching a trench.

"We did not lose a man in relieving," Duncan noted, "though the enemy fired much." Nervously, the young captain sprang to the parapet and planted the regimental colors.

Alexander Hamilton was not satisfied with fulfilling the letter of the siege regulations. In a booming voice, the twenty-six-year-old colonel ordered the entire regiment to mount the parapet, face the enemy, and there, to his bellowed orders, perform the manual of arms. The appalled Duncan was sure that the British would

blast them all into oblivion. But to the Captain's amazement, the enemy did not fire a shot. Hamilton knew his foes. The English would not dream of interrupting such bravado. It reminded them of their own British Guards, who in an earlier war had swaggered in front of the French lines and dared them to fire first.

The jittery Captain Duncan was not terribly impressed. Later he wrote in his diary that although he considered Colonel Hamilton "one of the first officers in the American army," he thought that he had recklessly exposed the lives of his men.

With the siege formally begun, Washington's chief worry was a British counterattack, or sortie. He kept 1,500 troops in the American wing trenches at all times and another 1,500 on the alert in ravines just behind them. The same caution prevailed in the French sector. Throughout the day, about eight hundred men sweated to build artillery emplacements and strengthen the redoubts. Sentries were ordered to watch the British lines constantly so that they could give an instant warning if they saw a mortar shell fired.

What value the amusingly misproportioned primitive at left possesses has more to do with who painted it than how skillfully he painted. This oil study of Washington at Yorktown was done by George Washington Parke Custis, whose father, Jack (one of two children of Martha Washington's first marriage), died of camp fever at Yorktown.

Fortunately, the mortar shells fired at Yorktown did not have the destructive force that shells of similar weight have today. The trenches were equipped with "blinds"—barrels filled with sand—behind which the men dived when a shell headed their way. The blinds were usually enough to protect them from the flying metal when the shell exploded. A projecting fuse gave the mortar shell a tumbling flight, which might last as long as ten seconds, while the fuse sputtered smoke and sparks. Sometimes the fuses kept on sputtering for a minute or two after the mortar shells hit. If the fuse burned too fast, the shell would explode in mid-air.

One mortar shell landed right in the middle of a sumptuous breakfast that Baron von Steuben was serving to his junior officers. Everyone dived for shelter and lay there until the shell exploded with a tremendous roar that showered the diners with mud and dirt but did not injure a man. The men were a little giddy at the narrow escape and began roaring with laughter at the muck on their faces and epaulets and breeches. The Baron's orderly produced some rum, and like veterans, they sat down to have another go at the breakfast.

Day and night during the seventh and eighth of October, the fatigue parties toiled on the vital gun platforms. Again and again their digging was interrupted by the sentry's cry: "A shell!" They all would dive behind the blinds, or just flatten themselves

80

Extremely realistic and rather fanciful elements are combined in thi[s] 1820 engraving of the siege. The artist's rendering of Yorktown itsel[f] (middle foreground) is considerably more imaginative than accurate, a[nd]

re the tightly grouped masses of infantry shown advancing on the left.
he siege cannon and mortars being fired on the right, however, are very
ccurately represented, as is the effectiveness of their repeated fire.

81

against the walls where they stood, and wait until the explosion sent its deadly fragments hissing through the air. Not a single American or French gun had yet fired a shot in answer to the British cannonade. This too was part of the formal theory of a siege that Washington was following. Besiegers did not open fire until they had enough batteries completed to outgun the enemy. Otherwise, the defenders could concentrate their fire and knock out the batteries one by one.

This was not much consolation for the men in the ranks. Day and night they had been digging and ducking, and the British fortifications still stood there, bristling with cannon and abatis, their sharpened points challenging a charge.

On October 9 this frustration finally ended. That morning, teams of oxen dragged big guns into position on the right flank, where the Americans were in charge, and on the left, before the British star redoubt, where the French were manning the trenches.

At 3 P.M. Washington gave the French battery on the far left permission to open fire. Some Americans groused at giving their allies this honor, but the French had completed their battery first and deserved the privilege.

The opening shots boomed down on the British ships in the harbor, especially the frigate *Guadaloupe*, which had been lying offshore, banging away at the French with her light cannon. She was no match for the heavy siege guns, and her captain hastily cut her cables and drifted with the current until his ship was out of range on the Gloucester side of the river.

The Americans soon forgot this minor French triumph in their excitement over the firing of their number one battery. On the platform were ten cannon—three twenty-four-pounders and three eighteen-pounders. There were also two eight-inch howitzers and two ten-and-a-half-inch mortars. These rode on carriages—invented by Henry Knox—that enabled them to fire on a horizontal line into the enemy's walls. It was hoped that the explosive shells would do more damage to Cornwallis' defenses than solid shot.

At five o'clock, the American standards were run up the flagpole, and General Washington himself put a long, glowing match to the touchhole. The first twenty-four-pound shot crashed through Yorktown. Colonel Philip Van Cortlandt of the Second New York Regiment later recalled that he could distinctly hear the ball "strike from house to house."

Both French and American guns began pouring mortar shells and solid shot into the town. The Americans' favorite target was the handsome Nelson house, which was Cornwallis' headquarters. They also worked over other houses suspected of containing British officers. Then the allied gunners switched to firing *en ricochet*—a technique that sent the balls skipping across the ground and up against the British gun embrasures. In a siege the

Siege weapons employed against the British garrisoned at Yorktown were of two basic types, both shown on the frontispiece of Muller's 1768 Treatise of Artillery. *Siege cannon, such as the one in the lower right foreground, were fired almost horizontally, to weaken and to eventually breach the city walls. Mortars (left foreground), on the other hand, were given a considerably higher trajectory, so that their shells would fall on targets deep within the city.*

enemy cannon were always prime targets. It was important to knock them out or at least reduce their fire to the point where they would be unable to interfere with the steady advance of the besiegers.

Washington ordered the artillery to blast away all night to prevent the British from repairing their damaged batteries. Lieutenant Ebenezer Denny thought that the bombardment from the allied side of the trenches was "grand." Mortar shells arched into the sky and tumbled down in long, curving trains of fire. Ball after ball of round shot tore into the soft, sandy earth of the British parapets or hummed through the town.

Two more French batteries opened up on the morning of the tenth, and the Americans began firing a second battery of four more eighteen-pounders and a third of two mortars. At least forty-six cannon were in action now. The average gun could fire about one hundred rounds a day. This meant

83

Painted fifteen years after the battle, Benjamin Latrobe's water color shows the still-vacant Nelson house (left, behind the city's walls) and the remains of a redoubt (lower right).

84

that there were approximately 4,600 shells and round shot pouring daily into the few thousand square yards of Virginia territory still under the control of the soldiers of King George.

"The whole of the batteries kept up an incessant fire," Washington noted in his diary. The Nelson house —and almost every other house—was soon a battered ruin, its windows knocked out, gaping holes in its roof, its chimneys heaps of scattered brick.

At about noon a white flag appeared on the American ramparts, and on both sides the guns ceased their murderous music. A messenger crossed no man's land and disappeared into the British works. After about a half hour, an old man hobbled out of the town gates. Many in the trenches recognized him instantly. It was "Secretary" Nelson. His two sons were in Washington's army, serving with the Virginia militia. When they saw the havoc the allied artillery was wreaking on their father's house, they had persuaded Washington to send the messenger into town, asking Cornwallis to let the old man go.

Cornwallis agreed, and soon the secretary was seated on a chair in Washington's tent, with American officers crowding around him, anxious to get the first real information on what the British were thinking and saying inside Yorktown.

The secretary reported that the American bombardment had been ferociously effective. Cornwallis and his staff were "burrowed in the ground" in a cave at the foot of the secretary's garden. Other officers were living in crude caves along the riverbank. The secretary himself had missed death by inches when a Negro servant standing beside him in his living room was killed by a cannon ball.

As soon as Nelson was safe in the American lines, the flag of truce came down and the big guns began blasting again. Meanwhile, other French and American troops were digging steadily, day and night, all along the siege line. First they would zig, then they would zag, then they would zig again, each twist carrying them a few more feet outside the main trench, closer to the British lines. On October 11, they were only 360 yards from the enemy parapets. To go farther would invite a British sortie—which could wipe them out before help from the main trench arrived. It was time to open the second parallel.

This was always the most delicate operation in a siege. Usually the enemy sortied to block or disrupt work on a second parallel. Once it was finished, the artillery would be moved in, so that the allies could open fire at three hundred yards—point-blank range. They would be able to pound Yorktown into rubble. The Americans were keenly aware of this. Adjutant General Edward Hand wrote a friend: "As soon as our batteries on the second parallel are completed, I think [the British] will begin to squeak."

Once more the French engineers laid out the line of the trench, and

when darkness fell, the sappers and miners and their well-armed covering parties crept stealthily forward. Lieutenant Feltman, who had eighty-two men in his command, said that every second man of the detachment carried a fascine and every man a shovel, spade, or grubbing hoe. They used them well. "Within an hour," Feltman said, "we had ourselves completely covered, so we disregarded their cannonading."

Surprise was complete in the American sector, but on the French wing the British heard some noise or were warned by a patrol. They unleashed a violent bombardment. The French artillery answered them, and the night was filled with thunder and the fiery tails of mortar shells. Some French guns fired over the American section of the line, and in the darkness a few fell short. "We were in the center of two fires, from the enemy and our own," Feltman noted wryly, "but the latter was very dangerous. We had two men killed and one badly wounded from the French batteries."

At some points the second parallel came within two hundred yards of the British ramparts. But it did not enclose the British left flank down to the riverbank, as the first parallel had done. Two British redoubts, numbered nine and ten, were advanced about two hundred yards in front of the main British line. They blocked the completion of the second parallel.

On the morning of October 12, when the British saw that the allies

Gruff but free-spending Baron von Steuben (above), painted "from life" by Ralph Earl in 1786, was responsible for the miraculously rapid training of the fledgling American army.

The slow siege irked Anthony Wayne (above, sketched by Trumbull), who favored the harrying tactics of earlier campaigns.

had advanced a giant step nearer Yorktown, all their guns went into action. Shots and shells rained on the American and French lines all morning, and casualties were unusually heavy. The mortar shells, particularly, could now be arched with deadly accuracy over the protective earthworks, and since they were fired from positions behind the walls, it was difficult for the allied artillery to knock them out. The French suffered nineteen casualties, and more men were lost when a shell dropped in the middle of a Virginia militia company.

Baron von Steuben seemed to attract mortar fire. Toward the end of the day, he and Brigadier General Anthony Wayne were in the second parallel trench when a sputtering shell came thudding to earth only a few feet away from them. Steuben instantly dived for the bottom of the trench, and Wayne followed him, landing on top of the Prussian drillmaster. The shell exploded with its usual shower of metal, and the Baron looked over his shoulder at Wayne. "I always knew you were brave, General," he said, "but I did not know you were perfect in every point of duty; you cover your General's retreat in the best manner possible."

Secretary Nelson had told the grim truth about the effect of the allied bombardment inside Yorktown. The British, convinced that the Americans had no heavy artillery, were totally unprepared for the ferocity of the fire. One of the first twenty-four-pound balls fired from American guns tore through the wooden walls of a house where the British commissary general and a group of officers were just sitting down to dinner. The missile screamed down the table, killing the commissary general and severely wounding three other officers.

The enlisted men were living in tents, several hundred feet behind the redoubts. Ten minutes of fire from the allied guns convinced them that they were nothing less than perfect targets, and there was a frantic rush to the safety of the trenches immediately behind the walls. The German soldier Stephan Popp betrayed his panic by wildly overestimating the weight of the allied mortars: "The enemy threw bombs, one hundred, one hundred and fifty, two hundred pounders. . . . A person could hardly stand the bombardment out of the town."

Yorktown's civilians were even more unprepared for the barrage. Worse, they had no place to hide. Corporal Popp reported that "the people fled to the waterside and hid in hastily contrived shelters on the banks, still they did not entirely escape, for many of them were fatally

Sure that the allies had no siege cannon, Cornwallis was astounded when the big guns opened up on Yorktown. This sketch from Charles Willson Peale's diary shows the gun carriages, designed by Knox, which permitted broadside fire at the city walls.

injured through the ricocheting of the bombs and howitzers, had arms or legs broken, or were killed."

Fortunately, there were few civilians left in Yorktown. On October 4, Cornwallis had decided to "turn out every nonessential mouth," to make sure that his food held out until Clinton arrived. Many of those he exiled were Negro slaves who had been lured from their Virginia masters on the British promise of freedom. Now self-preservation forced Cornwallis to renege. Most of these innocent victims of the war were ill with dysentery, smallpox, and malaria. Bewildered and afraid, they wandered in the woods around the allied camp, starving to death or dying of disease.

But food was not Cornwallis' chief worry—his greatest problem was ammunition. To slow the progress of a

GLOUCESTER
POINT

YORK

RIVER

RIVER

A CHART
of the JAMES and YORK
RIVERS
in VIRGINIA
from Cape Henry
to James Island

WILLIAMSBURG

JAMES RIVER

WILLIAMSBURG NECK

YORK RIVER

CHESAPEAK BAY

besieging army, the defenders had to be able to pour vast quantities of shot and shell on the enemy. On October 4, naval Lieutenant Bartholomew James sadly noted in his journal, "We kept up as heavy a fire on them as our want of ammunition would allow."

The tenth of October was a bitter day inside Yorktown. By evening British battery number five, commanded by the first lieutenant of the *Charon*, was knocked out by the allied counterfire. The lieutenant and his men "quit" the battery, James said, "the shot and shell having dismounted his guns and tore up his platform." That night the French fired "hot shot" (cannon balls heated in a furnace) at the *Charon* and set her afire. She and three smaller ships in the harbor burned to the water line.

From dusk to dawn the allied artillery poured metal on the British. Sleep was impossible. There was constant skirmishing outside the works between allied and British patrols.

To guard against a surprise attack, each night the British stationed sentries outside their ramparts, in no man's land. The enlisted men hated the assignment. Another German soldier, Johann Doehla, gives a vivid

By September 10, increasingly accurate allied gunfire had knocked out several of the British forward gun emplacements. Firing "hot shot"—furnace-heated cannon balls—from their mortars, the allies set the Charon *(center) afire off Gloucester Point and drove the* Guadaloupe *northward.*

picture of his duty during the night of October 5:

I went on duty at a detached picket which was outside our lines. It was dangerous on this picket post; one had either to sit or lie the two hours one stood post, so that he could not be seen against the starry sky from the enemy's outposts, which often stood scarcely 5–600 paces distance from us. When it was quiet one could hear every relieving of watch and patrols; and now French, now English or German calling out: "Who's there?" "Friend.". . . Throughout the night the location of the post is altered in order that the enemy might observe the less. Everything must proceed quietly. One dares call out neither to sentry nor patrol except to give only the agreed signal. Nor does one dare smoke tobacco nor make a fire. The men call it the "lost post" with all justice.

According to Lieutenant James, the German regiments panicked several times and fled the trenches. They had to be driven back at gunpoint.

The Hessian regiment was in the second line of defense, considerably behind the front trenches. This made it a prime target for allied artillery. Almost every hour a man was killed or wounded. The British light infantry, who were manning the "hornwork"—the foremost line of the British defense—took even heavier casualties. They were blasted from both flanks by the French and the American gunners. Before the siege was over, they were to lose four lieutenants, five sergeants, and seventy-five rank and file—the heaviest casualties of Yorktown.

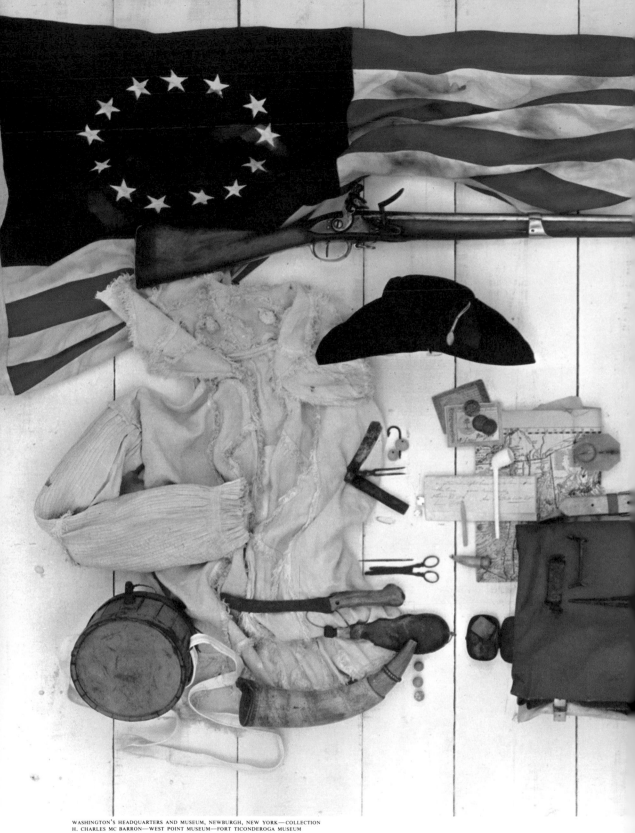

*Few Continentals were fortunate enough to hav
a full uniform, but those who had wore a blu
coat with white facings over buff leggings an
waistcoat (right). Riflemen wore the fringe*

hirt and tricorn hat at left, and both carried French muskets similar to the one shown above. In general, equipment varied with the individual soldier's needs and resources and might include such items as (left center, clockwise from top): Continental currency, compass, clay pipe (all on the map), ice-creepers (on the red knapsack), powderhorn, shot pouch, and personal utensils.

"I now want words," Lieutenant James wrote in his journal for October 11, "to express the dreadful situation of the garrison." Houses collapsed or exploded into flames. Cries of wounded and dying men echoed above the constant thunder of the cannon fire. There was simply no place to hide. The scene, James said, was enough to "fill every mind with pity and compassion." Yet surrender was still a forbidden word.

Amidst all this dire destruction [James said], no murmuring was heard, no wish to give up the town while the most distant hope was in view of being relieved. On the contrary, this very distinguished little army, taking example from their chief, went through the business of the siege with a perfect undaunted resolution and

Muller's contemporary water-color studies of Hessian mercenaries include this one of members of von Wurmb's Jäger Corps.

hourly discovered proofs of their attachment to the general, who had so often led them to the field with success.

Cornwallis always made a point of sharing the sufferings of his men. On his march through the Carolinas, he had slept in the fields with them and eaten the same poor rations. Now, ignoring the allied fire, he was constantly in the trenches, ordering guns to be shifted or directing the construction of a battery to replace one that had been knocked out. Such a general inspired young men to volunteer for the post of danger, and this is what Lieutenant James did on the morning of October 12. The sailors from the transports had been manning the batteries in the hornwork, but that day they grew panicky at their heavy casualties and quit. James offered to replace them.

Had James not been a veteran of the point-blank artillery duels of naval warfare, he could never have endured the next eight hours. At least sixty-two allied guns were now in action, and only a handful of British batteries were left to fire back. When Lieutenant James, his midshipman, and thirty-six seamen opened up with their battery of seven guns, almost every cannon in the allied lines zeroed in on them. He vividly described the scene:

Fifty-two minutes after my arrival in the hornwork, the enemy silenced the three left guns by closing the embrasures, shortly after which they dismounted a twelve pounder, knocked off the muzzles of two eighteens, and for the last hour and a half left me with one eighteen pounder with a part of its muzzle also shot away.

The carnage among James' men was even more awful. Nine men were killed instantly. Of twenty-eight wounded, eight died before they could be moved. Every man that came with him in the morning was a casualty by nightfall. "Most of the wounded," James said tersely, "had lost an arm or a leg, and some both."

That same day, a daring British major, Charles Cochrane, slipped through the French fleet in a whale boat. He arrived with a message from Sir Henry Clinton canceling all his rosy promises and telling Cornwallis that the British fleet could not sail from New York with a relief expedition until October 12, if then.

Cornwallis' answer was grim. The impact of the allied bombardment had already destroyed his optimism. He told Clinton that he was losing men "very fast" and that many of his works were "seriously damaged." Against so powerful an attack, he could not hope "to make a very long resistance."

Soon after Cochrane's arrival, Cornwallis received some unsolicited advice from his senior officers. According to Banastre Tarleton, they told him he should "evacuate the miserable works of York Town where every hour of day and night was an hour of watching and danger to the officer and soldier, where every gun was dismounted as soon as shown . . ."

Muller also painted the less-fortunate Regiment Knyphausen, which was captured during the Battle of Trenton in 1776.

The officers argued that a retreat by night to the Gloucester side and a breakout from there could achieve a headstart "of one hundred miles distance . . . by rapid marches" before Washington could organize a pursuit.

Cornwallis listened impassively to this suggestion and then returned a regretful *no*. Sir Henry Clinton must give him a positive order before he could in conscience evacuate the post. Although Sir Henry had mentioned many circumstances that might delay him, the commander in chief still said that he was coming south to relieve Yorktown. Until that plan was dropped, he did not feel free to retreat.

6

ASSAULT ON YORKTOWN

It was the end of the second week in October, and the allies still had not completed the second parallel. The two forward British redoubts (numbers nine and ten) stood squarely in the middle of the last four hundred yards of trench that the allied engineers had sketched on their maps. The ever-present threat of de Grasse's October 30 deadline made it imperative to take these positions by storm.

Crusty Baron de Viomenil, second in command of the French forces, had asked Rochambeau to let him attack the redoubts even before the parallel was dug. On October 14 Rochambeau told the artillery to cease firing, and with his son, Vicomte de Rochambeau, who served as his aide, he climbed out of the trench and strolled coolly down a gully to the nearest redoubt's outer works. His staff officers,

Unable to reduce two of the British forward redoubts by bombardment during the first five days of the siege, the allies were forced to take them by storm. Eugene Lami's painting (a detail of which appears on the cover) shows Americans replacing the Union Jack with the Stars and Stripes.

97

as nervous as were Washington's, feared for his life, but the English did not fire a shot at him.

The portly French General came back and told Viomenil that he would have to wait a little longer for his assault. "The outer works and the palisades are still intact," he said. "We shall have to double our fire to break them and knock down the parapet. We shall see tomorrow if the pear is ripe."

The allied artillery spent the rest of the day pounding the two redoubts. They maintained almost as fierce a fire on the star-shaped redoubt held by the Royal Welsh Fusiliers on the opposite side of the peninsula. By giving both ends of the battle line equal punishment, Washington was playing his favorite game of keeping the British guessing.

At two P.M. the engineers reported to Washington that by nightfall the British positions would be so heavily damaged that a successful assault could be made. Washington immediately ordered Lafayette to select four hundred of his toughest light infantrymen for the job. For their target, the General chose redoubt number ten, the one on the edge of the riverbank. He gave Rochambeau the freedom to choose the best of his own troops for the simultaneous French attack on redoubt number nine.

Lafayette entrusted the leadership of the American assault to the Chevalier de Gimat, his former aide, who had come to America with him in 1777.

When Alexander Hamilton heard this news, he protested violently. Hamilton told his good friend Lafayette that he was senior colonel to Gimat, and moreover, that the attack would take place during his tour of duty in the lines. Even though Lafayette was a major general, Hamilton complained, he had no right to replace him. Embarrassed, Lafayette tried to avoid the argument by saying that it was now too late to change the arrangements. Washington had already approved them.

Hamilton refused to give up. He wrote a bold letter to Washington demanding this highly dangerous assignment for himself. Washington told an aide to check the facts and discovered that Hamilton was right about the tour of duty and was also senior to Gimat in his commission. The commander in chief ordered Lafayette to give Hamilton the command of the American assault. Gimat would have to be satisfied with the leadership of an infantry battalion in the attack.

Later in the day Washington rode to the French camp and conferred with Baron de Viomenil. The commander in chief was amused, and pleased, to learn that there were a number of "Hamiltons" in the French army. The Baron was being bombarded with pleas from at least a dozen young officers who wanted to participate in the attack.

Viomenil had chosen Lieutenant Colonel William de Deux-Ponts to lead the French assault. As he and his men filed into the trenches, they

In Trumbull's delicate preliminary pencil sketch for his surrender scene (shown on pages 142–143), the subject, Comte de Deux-Ponts, is almost overwhelmed by notations on the French officer's uniform.

heard a voice calling to them: *"Auvergne, Auvergne sans tache."* It was General Rochambeau himself, making an emotional appeal to his old regiment, which he had led across so many European battlefields. "My children," he said, "I have great need of you tonight. I trust you will not forget that we have served together in the brave Regiment of Auvergne, surnamed *Auvergne sans tache*—the spotless."

At the head of the trench, Deux-Ponts was joined by some unexpected volunteers. The Chevalier de Lameth was risking the wrath of Rochambeau to participate in the assault. Rochambeau had sternly refused his request to join it, but the young daredevil went anyway. With him were Comte Charles de Damas, who had not even bothered to ask his General's permission, and Comte de Vauban, who had been sent by Rochambeau as an observer but now insisted on joining the ranks. "I tried to turn them back," Deux-Ponts later recalled, "but they would not pay heed to the protest that I made—which would have withdrawn them from the field of glory and of honor."

Washington, meanwhile, satisfied with the French dispositions, rode back to his waiting Americans. At first glance, the four hundred men in their ragged shirts and ruined shoes did not look like the equals of the superbly equipped French grenadiers and chasseurs that he had just left. But he had complete confidence in their fighting ability. Most of them had seen five years of war. They were lean, tough, professional soldiers now. Although Washington was not the sort of general who ordinarily gave speeches, he gave a short one to these men. He urged them to be firm and brave; the success of the attack on both redoubts depended on them.

Washington had good reason to worry. Both attacks must succeed, or both would fail. If the British retained one of the forward redoubts, they could easily pour troops into it and overwhelm the captured one before the allies could support it. Reinforcements then would have to run a gantlet of point-blank fire from the alerted British cannoneers on the inner parapets. Once the attack was repulsed, the British would cram the redoubts with troops and make a second attack impossible. Washington would be forced to revise his entire strategy, and the siege would be delayed by three or four precious days.

Among the men who were deeply moved by Washington's speech was Stephen Olney, the young captain of a Rhode Island light infantry company. He and his men were to form the head of one attacking column. "I thought then," he said, "that His Excellency's knees rather shook, but I have since doubted whether it was not mine."

As the twilight deepened, Baron de Viomenil began to have second thoughts about using the American troops in the attack. He had urged that the job be done entirely by the French, with the Americans following only to mop up. Washington had politely rejected the idea; he knew that his soldiers would consider it an insult to American honor.

The Baron found Lafayette and repeated his worries about the Americans. Lafayette had difficulty in controlling his temper; he was proud of his rank in the American army and equally proud of his men. To put the Baron in his place, he replied calmly: "We are young soldiers and have only one way in these cases. That is to unload our guns and march right in with

No Revolutionary figure was more infamous than the turncoat Benedict Arnold, whose raiding party massacred American prisoners at New London in September, 1781. An appropriately two-faced effigy, accompanied by the Devil, had been paraded through Philadelphia and burned a year before. The exhibit, but not the woodcut of the scene above, was made by C. W. Peale.

our bayonets." The Marquis promptly ordered Hamilton and his men to empty their muskets. Viomenil withdrew, a chastened general.

Darkness approached, and the waiting Americans fingered their bayonets and talked broodingly of news that had reached the army only a few days before. Early in September, while they were marching south, Benedict Arnold had led a British raid on New London, and the British had slaughtered dozens of American militiamen in one of the town's forts—after they had surrendered. More than a few of the battle-toughened New Englanders swore that they were going to get their revenge before the night was over.

At about seven-thirty P.M.—just when darkness became complete— there was a crackle of muskets on the extreme left of the allied line, soon followed by the thunder of cannon. The French regiments were faking an attack on the Fusiliers' redoubt to distract the British. Then, at exactly eight o'clock, the guns from the French Grand Battery gave the long-awaited signal, and six mortars were fired in quick succession.

Armed with an axe, Sergeant Joseph Plumb Martin of the sappers and miners was in the front ranks of the American attackers. The light infantrymen were depending on them to cut a path through the abatis so that they could storm the redoubt itself.

"The two brilliant planets, Jupiter and Venus, were in close contact in the western hemisphere," Martin said,

and he was so tense that more than once he almost sprang to his feet, thinking that they were blazing mortar shells signaling the attack. Then the guns fired, and the words "Up! Up!" were barked through the ranks. "Our watchword was Rochambeau," Martin said, "a good watchword, for being pronounced Ro-Sham-Bow, it sounded, when pronounced quick, like Rush-on-boys."

The light infantrymen divided into two columns, Hamilton commanding one and his ex-rival Colonel Gimat leading the other. Beside Gimat was another daring French volunteer, the Marquis de La Rouërie. Captain Stephen Olney and his Rhode Islanders were only a few steps behind the two Frenchmen. "The column marched in silence, with guns unloaded and in good order," Olney wrote. "Many no doubt thinking that less than one-quarter of a mile would finish the journey of life with them." A good officer, Olney did his best to encourage several men who looked as if they might desert, whispering that he had "full confidence" in their courage.

Halfway to the redoubt, the column halted, and one man was selected from each company for the "forlorn hope." These men would be the first over the wall. Almost certain to meet desperate resistance, they were supposed to draw enemy fire and clear away any unexpected obstructions for the main body of attackers on their heels. Only the best and bravest soldiers were chosen for this risky but

Reuben Reed's painting of Washington and Lafayette at Yorktown was based on a description given him by an eyewitness. Apparently untroubled by the lack of perspective and unmenacing fireworks, the veteran pronounced himself pleased by the canvas' "realistic effect."

vital job. "My men all seemed ready to go," Olney proudly noted.

Once more, the column moved into the night, the sappers in front, the "forlorn hope" next, then Gimat, Rouërie, and six or eight officer volunteers. In tension-filled silence they reached the British outer defenses without a challenge from redoubt number ten. For a moment they hesitated before the abatis, which had not been as damaged by the artillery fire as the allied engineers had assumed that it would be. In the same instant, from the wall of the redoubt, a sentry demanded the password. He received

no answer. A moment later the night exploded, as, in Olney's words, "the enemy fired a full volley of musketry."

"At this our men broke silence and huzzaed," Olney wrote, "and as the order for silence seemed broken by everyone, I huzzaed with all my power, saying how frightened [the British] are, they fire right into the air."

Not all the British were so jittery. Several men, including Colonel Gimat, were hit by the first volley. The Frenchman was carried out of the battle, his foot bloodied by a musket ball. The sappers began hacking away at the abatis. The excited light infantry decided, Captain Olney said, that "This seemed tedious work in the dark within three rods of the enemy." Whooping and howling, they stormed past Sergeant Martin and the other sappers, crawled and twisted through and around the pointed stakes, and poured down on the redoubt, shouting, "Rush on boys, Rush on boys, the fort's our own!"

The battle cry drew another volley of British musketry. Abandoning his axe-work, Sergeant Joseph Plumb Martin joined the race and saw men disappearing all around him. "I thought the British were killing us off at a great rate," he wrote. Then he tumbled head-first into a huge hole torn up by an allied mortar shell. Scrambling out, he found dozens of other men peering dazedly out of similar holes nearby. Thus he discovered "the mystery of the huge slaughter."

In the trench just underneath the British breastwork, Martin recognized an old friend from the light infantry. "I knew him by the light of the enemy's musketry, it was so vivid." Captain Olney already had crawled up on the parapet and found an opening ripped in the palisades by a cannon ball. He stepped in, calling: "Captain Olney's company form here."

Olney immediately found himself in a duel to the death with six lunging bayonets. "I parried as well as I could with my espontoon," he recalled. But the blade of this now-forgotten officer's weapon (a sort of spear) broke off, and "their bayonets slipped along the handle of my espontoon and scaled my fingers." One bayonet gouged Olney's thigh, another pierced his abdomen just above the hip. A third redcoat fired at him point-blank, and the blast flung the Captain back against the palisades, convinced that his arm had been torn off.

With a last-ditch thrust, Captain Olney caught his attacker in the forehead with the remains of his espontoon. Two of Olney's men, John Strange and Benjamin Bennet, leaped up on the parapet beside him. They had decided that Lafayette's boast about empty muskets was idiocy and had stopped to load their guns. They fired a blast at Olney's attackers, who either ran away or surrendered.

A few feet away, the stumpy Hamilton had trouble getting up on the parapet, until two nearby men gave him a boost. Behind him, light infantrymen all but trampled each other in their fury to get inside the redoubt. The British hurled primitive hand grenades among their attackers, but the crackling and popping of these weapons, designed more to frighten than to wound, went totally ignored. Sergeant Martin reported that the sappers and miners disobeyed their commanding officer, Captain James Gilliland, and shouted that they were going inside too, even if they had only axes with which to defend themselves.

"We will go," they roared.

"Then go to the devil," Gilliland roared back and went with them.

Unlike many painters of Yorktown scenes, Louis Van Blarenberghe was an eyewitness to the siege—a fact reflected in the painting above, which shows the sheltered "ways" (center) leading into the silent first parallel (middleground) and the now extremely active second parallel beyond.

Martin tried to fight his way through an entrance that he and several other sappers had chopped in the palisades, but the surging infantrymen shouldered him aside. He ran to another place, where artillery fire had blown away a few of the stakes. "While passing, a man at my side received a ball in the head, and fell under my feet, crying out bitterly." There were no medics to help the wounded at Yorktown; the man would

104

have to wait until his comrades finished their grim work inside the fort.

There was no time to load guns. Lafayette's boast about the bayonet was coming close to the truth as the British and Germans thrust and parried with the Americans in the tumultuous darkness. German oaths and British curses were swallowed by the growing howl of American triumph.

Some of the British had decided early that the game was up. The defenders of one flank of the redoubt fled even before Captain Olney made his one-man assault over the parapet. Ironically, the panicky British in retreat collided with the Americans who were supposed to assault that point. The redcoats bayoneted some of the attackers and sent the other light infantrymen fleeing, convinced that they were objects of a British counterattack. "I asked one of the others how he did not get into the redoubt," Olney recalled later. "He said the enemy pricked them off with their bayonets." Several other not-so-brave redcoats escaped by sliding down the almost perpendicular riverbank and fleeing along the beach to the town.

From all sides the Americans were now swamping the defenders. When Colonel John Laurens and eighty men boiled over the rear wall, Major Campbell, the British commander of the redoubt, realized that further resistance would only waste lives. He handed his sword to the dashing South Carolinian. Campbell himself was wounded, and his sixty men were outnumbered by seven to one. His Hessian and British soldiers dropped their muskets and asked for quarter. Victory had been won in little more than five minutes. Nine Americans were dead, and twenty-five wounded.

The Marquis de Lafayette, waiting tensely in the first parallel trench, sent an aide to Baron de Viomenil to announce that the Americans had captured redoubt number ten—and to ask if the French needed any help in carrying number nine. Lafayette later admitted that he enjoyed "unspeakable satisfaction" when he sent this message to the condescending Baron. Viomenil had to confess that the French did not yet possess redoubt number nine—but they soon would.

The French were behind schedule because, as well-trained professional soldiers, they had waited for their sappers to cut away the abatis in front of their objective. This cost them men

as well as time. The defenders, one hundred twenty veteran troops of the Hessian Regiment de Bose, poured volley after volley into the French. Although men toppled left and right, they stood their ground like the veterans they were. "Before starting," Colonel de Deux-Ponts said, "I had ordered that no one should fire before reaching the crest of the parapet of the redoubt; and when established upon the parapet, that no one should jump into the works before receiving the orders to do so." Deux-Ponts and his men found the abatis "strong and well preserved," twenty-five paces from their objective. Here, too, the engineers had been overoptimistic about the artillery's power.

It took five cruel minutes to reach the outer trench, and there they waited again for the eight sappers to hack at the palisades. The more daring grenadiers and chasseurs fought their way up onto the parapet to find—or claw—their own openings. In this Gallic melée the veteran Lieutenant Colonel D'Estrade—sent along to make sure that the younger Deux-Ponts made no mistakes—came to grief. Just as he planted both feet on the parapet, a soldier grabbed him by his coattails and sent him spinning back down into the ditch. About two hundred men trampled him underfoot before the battered Colonel managed to stagger to his feet and fight his way forward.

The German defenders met the men on the wall with another volley. The fiery young Chevalier de Lameth toppled back into the ditch, both knees shattered. Captain de Sireuil crumpled with a mangled leg. Lieutenant de Sillegue of the chasseurs turned to hoist Deux-Ponts to the top and dropped with a mortal wound just as the Colonel reached his side.

The parapet nevertheless continued to fill with determined French grenadiers, and the desperate Hessians fell back behind the barrels that they had been using to protect themselves against mortar shells. The barrels were no protection against the French fire from the parapet, however. "All our shots told," Deux-Ponts grimly remarked.

If the Germans had fought a moment longer, the Count would have ordered a bayonet charge to finish them off. But the defenders threw down their guns and asked for quarter. *"Vive le roi!"* shouted Deux-Ponts, and the men around him took up the victory cry. Soon all the men in the trenches were echoing it.

"The enemy replied by a general discharge of artillery and musketry," Deux-Ponts recalled. "I never saw a sight more beautiful or more majestic." Fearful that a general assault was about to take place, the British ordered a "roulade"—rolling fire down their whole line—designed to do maximum damage to attackers as they sprang from their trenches.

The French had suffered 114 casualties—46 dead and 68 wounded— and reinforcements were rushed into the redoubt to bolster the depleted assault wave. Washington and Rochambeau expected the British to counterattack in a desperate effort to retake the lost redoubts.

While the British blasted away at men who were not there, Deux-Ponts was shouting orders to get his wounded out of the redoubt and back to the hospital. A nervous sentry thought that he saw the British counterattack coming and cried an alarm. Deux-Ponts peered over the parapet after the fellow's pointing finger. At that moment a cannon ball ricocheted past him, flinging sand and stones in Deux-Ponts's eyes, blinding and stunning him. He had to be led to the hospital, and almost a week passed before he recovered his sight and hearing.

George Washington was waiting just behind the lines, standing in an exposed spot. When the British began firing their roulade, one of his aides, Colonel David Cobb, begged him to move to a safer position. The tense Washington did not take the warning with his usual good humor. "If you are afraid, Colonel Cobb," he snapped, "you may retire."

The men of the Pennsylvania Line had been waiting in reserve under the command of Colonel Richard Butler. The moment the two redoubts were secured, they flung aside their guns, seized picks and shovels, and began digging toward the victors to complete the second parallel trench. The British knew what they were doing and tried to stop them with all the artillery they had left. But the dark-

Chief of artillery and a steadfast friend of Washington's, jovial Henry Knox later was the nation's first Secretary of War.

ness protected the Americans; most of the shells went over their heads.

The French, in their section of the second parallel, were not so lucky; there, a British battery found the range, killing twenty-seven men and sending one hundred nine wounded staggering back to the hospital. By the end of the night, the distraught Commissary Blanchard had more than five hundred sick and wounded on his hands—and still not enough medicine or supplies to care for them properly.

By morning the digging Pennsylvanians had reached the two captured redoubts, and the second parallel was complete. That same morning, October 15, Washington visited the redoubts. Musket balls hissed near him, for the trenches were now close enough to Yorktown's inner defenses for soldiers to exchange fire easily. Again Washington ignored the danger, and his aides fretted. The General approved his engineers' decision to build two new artillery batteries, which would be connected to the captured redoubts. By that afternoon the Americans had dragged two howitzers inside the former British bastions.

In a letter to the President of the Continental Congress, Washington explained the importance of these two redoubts once they were armed with allied cannon. "From them," he wrote, "we shall enfilade the enemy's whole line and I am in hopes we shall be able to command the communication from York to Gloucester." By "enfilade," Washington meant that they could pour round shot and shell down the length of the British forward trenches, making them untenable. It was the last step before the climax of every siege—the general assault.

After writing a report that generously praised the bravery of his men, Alexander Hamilton returned to the captured redoubt with Major General Henry Knox, who was supervising the construction of the new batteries. The

108

cocky young Colonel began criticizing Washington's order to sound a warning when a mortar shell was fired. It was unsoldierly, even cowardly to have officers and men constantly diving behind barrels, Hamilton argued. Why not ignore the fire, just as a soldier does in a frontal assault?

Knox snorted with indignation and told Hamilton that Washington was trying to save the lives of the men. Hamilton, displaying the brilliant eloquence that he would later use to overpower judges and juries, was winning the argument with Knox when a sentry cried: "A shell!" Moments later, two fizzling British mortar shells landed only a few feet away. Hamilton and Knox dived for the protection of some nearby blinds. They arrived simultaneously, and Hamilton, seizing Knox, spun him around so that the artilleryman's bulk was between him and the sputtering bombs.

With a squawk of rage, Knox sent Hamilton whirling off his back and out from behind the blinds toward the still-hissing shells. Hamilton scrambled back, and a minute later the shells went off. Both men were untouched by the flying fragments. But Hamilton had lost the argument and could only look sheepish while Knox lectured him.

"Now what do you think, Mr. Hamilton, about crying shell? But let me tell you not to make a breastwork of me again!"

Elsewhere, the grim business of the siege went on. The allied cannon continued to slam home shots and shells by the thousands. Now there was not a single British cannon able to answer. Only the mortars, sheltered from the direct fire of the allied batteries, kept up a feeble fire.

Teams of men and horses dragged more guns into action. The Americans now had a "grand battery" consisting of twelve twenty-fours and eighteens, plus four mortars and two howitzers. "The whole peninsula," one American noted in his journal, "trembles under the incessant thunder of our infernal machines." At five P.M. on October 15, the mortars that had been dragged into the captured redoubts opened fire, dropping their deadly bombs almost literally into the laps of the British troops in the forward trenches. On the next day they would be joined by a full battery of cannon.

Close to one hundred guns would be in action then, capable of flinging ten thousand rounds a day into Yorktown. The moment was approaching when Cornwallis' troops, with all their guns silenced and the walls shattered by the artillery, would be stormed. Another day, two at the most, would bring the signal, and the waves of French and American infantry would spring from the second parallel for the final furious dash across the two hundred yards that separated them from victory.

The British faced certain, catastrophic defeat—unless Sir Henry Clinton or Charles Lord Cornwallis had a final card to play.

7

THE LAST GAMBLE

In New York Sir Henry Clinton could only fret and fume. Admiral Thomas Graves insisted that the ships mauled by de Grasse could not sail until every splintered spar had been replaced, every last damaged plank in every hull restored. Finally, on October 12, Graves reported that the fleet was ready, and Clinton put every available soldier on board the men of war. If they sailed on the next day, with good weather they could easily reach the Chesapeake by October 17.

The thirteenth of October dawned fair and warm, with a soft breeze out of the southwest. But around noon a huge black cloud appeared in the western sky, and minutes later a small hurricane exploded over New York harbor. For an hour and a half, rain mixed with hail pelted men and ships, while thunder boomed and lightning ripped the sky. A northwest wind howled through the rigging, and anchor cables groaned as they were strained to the snapping point. Then came disaster. The *Alcide* parted her cable, and with a shocking crunch, smashed into the *Shrewsbury*, demol-

ishing her bowsprit and springing the *Alcide*'s own foreyard.

Two days later, on October 15, the entire fleet was still waiting off Staten Island while the *Shrewsbury* was fitted with a new bowsprit. On the sixteenth some ships of the line tried to move from the upper river to Staten Island, but the wind was against them and they had to anchor once more. Yet another day had been lost.

By this time, the situation was desperate in Yorktown. Part of the British garrison was near mutiny. Every day Johann Doehla recorded new desertions in his diary; his own regiment had lost almost fifty men. A deserter told the Americans of one British regiment that refused to do its duty in the lines until Lord Cornwallis gave them an extra ration of wine and promised them that the fleet would arrive soon to relieve them.

Possibly Cornwallis himself no longer believed that help would come.

Finished in 1783, this striking portrait by Thomas Gainsborough shows Cornwallis some two years after his return to England.

110

ARLES EARL CORNWALLIS. 1783.

Louis Marie, Vicomte de Noailles

His letter of October 15 to Sir Henry Clinton was a frank statement of impending collapse. He told Clinton that his situation had become "very critical." His forces could no longer show a gun to the allied batteries, and his works were being battered into crumbling ruins. His "bad position and weakened numbers" gave Cornwallis small hope of repelling an assault, which he expected at any moment. It would be foolish, he concluded, for Sir Henry and the fleet to "run great risk" in trying to save them.

But Lord Cornwallis was not the kind of man who collapsed when his troubles multiplied. At a midnight conference, he and his officers decided to attempt a sortie to spike some of the allied cannon. They might even gain control of the second parallel trench itself. With luck they could then silence other batteries.

Lieutenant Colonel Robert Abercromby was told to select three hundred fifty good men for the sortie. The men were ordered to rely solely on the bayonet and to concentrate more on spiking cannon than on fighting enemy troops. Every man knew that it was a desperate but necessary gamble. Another day's cannonade from the second parallel was at least as dangerous and far more nerve-racking to endure.

At three A.M. Abercromby led his picked troops into the hornwork. For their attack they chose the junction of the French and American sections of the trenches. They shrewdly judged that this point would not be as carefully guarded as some other parts of the allied line. In addition, there were two batteries of artillery within easy striking distance—an American one to the left, a French to the right.

Without a single sentry challenging them, the attackers reached the main trench of the second parallel. There they split into two groups. In the French battery the officer and most of the fifty men of the Agenais Regiment were asleep. The British marched boldly toward them, telling a sentry that they were an American relief detachment. Then, at a growled order, they charged, bayoneting some of the sleepers and sending the survivors fleeing for their lives. The British let them go and went to work at spiking the cannon.

The American battery to be attacked was guarded by one hundred

Virginia militiamen armed only with picks and shovels; they had stacked their guns outside the redoubt. When a sentry challenged them, the British used the same ruse that had succeeded against the French battery:

"What troops?" asked the Americans.

In this French lithograph, an apparently unperturbed Washington, arms folded across his chest (right rear), watches a frenzied American assault force overrun a redoubt.

"French," was the reply, and the British moved coolly forward. At the moment that their red uniforms gave them away, their commander howled, "Push on my brave boys and skin the bastards!"

Colonel Henry Skipwith, the American commander, kept his head. He told his men to get out of the redoubt as fast as possible and find their guns. The British wasted no time on the fleeing militiamen; it was the cannon that

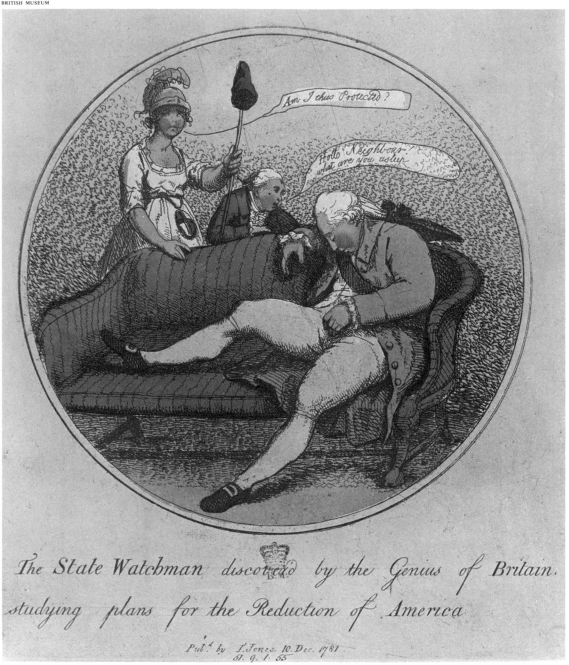

Confused British reaction to news of the Yorktown disaster is reflected in Thomas Rowland-son's cartoon, which was published on December 10, 1781, just fifteen days after the news reached England. In it, an incredulous Britannia and a befuddled George III discover that Lord North—as Prime Minister, its "Watchman"—has slept complacently through the crisis.

they were after. Before they could do a professional spiking job, however, aroused French grenadiers under Lafayette's brother-in-law, the Vicomte de Noailles, poured into both redoubts, crying, *"Vive le roi!"*

With no quarter asked or given, a fierce bayonet fight erupted in the predawn darkness. The outnumbered British began to fall back, but one tough sergeant refused to retreat, even when it was obvious that the French were about to cut him off. The sergeant finally fell with a dozen wounds, while behind him his comrades streamed back to the British lines, with a captured French officer as a prize for their daring.

Colonel Richard Butler admired the "secrecy and spirit" with which the British had executed the sortie, but Washington in his diary dismissed it as "small and ineffectual . . . of little consequence to either party." Both judgments were sound.

The British had not succeeded in knocking out the big guns. In order to ruin an eighteenth-century cannon, a metal wedge had to be hammered into its touchhole—where the powder, which ignites the charge, is inserted—so tightly that not even a blacksmith could get it out without melting down the entire gun. The attackers had time only to jam in their bayonets and break off the points as a stopgap measure.

Allied engineers and artillerymen toiled all morning to clear the touchholes. By noon, every gun was back in firing condition, and the relentless bombardment was renewed with increased fury. Johann Doehla noted that one battery of fourteen guns was so close to the hornwork "that one could nearly throw stones into it." Stephan Popp said that it was worse than any fire that they had yet received. It seemed to him "as though the heavens should split." Everyone expected that the final storm—"to finish us off"—would take place momentarily.

By now almost two thousand sick and wounded were in the British hospitals. They, too, had no shelter from the rain of metal. That afternoon, Stephan Popp said, the enemy firing was "almost unendurable." Worse, the young German could see the allied working parties building a huge battery of ten mortars and twenty-four-pound cannons on the right flank of the British line. When these opened up at second-parallel range, no one would be able to raise his head in Yorktown and survive.

At last, Lord Cornwallis decided to take the advice that his senior officers had offered a week before. In his dugout headquarters during the afternoon of October 16, Cornwallis huddled with his staff, working out a plan to cross the York River and smash their way to freedom from their less heavily invested camp at the neighboring town of Gloucester.

As soon as darkness fell, the British regiments were to be quietly withdrawn from the front lines and ferried

Directly across the river from Yorktown, but almost unaffected by the siege, was Glouceste
the rallying point for troops ferried across the York River during Cornwallis' unsuccessf
breakout attempt on the night of October 16. When a sudden squall thwarted their escap

e British pulled back to Yorktown, leaving the Gloucester post under Banastre Tarleton's mmand. Surrendered unscathed two days later, the port looked much as it had in 1755, hen a British officer painted this companion piece to the scene of Yorktown on pages 36–37.

across the river. The Germans would follow them. Using every available boat, the men who were still in fighting condition could make it across in three trips. In Gloucester, Banastre Tarleton was ordered to prepare his cavalrymen and gather every horse. Tarleton responded with enthusiasm. On the chance that Cornwallis would take his advice, he already had contacted a loyalist who knew a secret path from which Tarleton could surprise the Duc de Lauzun's legion from the rear.

The breakout attempt was to begin at dawn. The British army would surge from the Gloucester works, sweeping before it the French marines and the American militia. Tarleton would either annihilate or scatter Lauzun's legion. The British dragoons would seize the French horses and mount as many infantrymen as possible, two on a horse. Commandeering more horses and food from towns and farms along their route, they would lead a forced march up the peninsula into Maryland. Their eventual goal would be New York. But they could improvise other plans—perhaps striking out for the coast in the hopes of finding the British relieving fleet.

All the wounded and sick were to be left in Yorktown. Lieutenant James and his fellow sailors from the fleet were to man the ramparts through the night and into the dawn. The moment the army broke out of Gloucester, Yorktown was to run up a white flag.

118

As a matter of necessity in time of battle, the hierarchy of power and privilege on board a British ship of war was absolute. How obvious those distinctions were can be readily seen in the three ink sketches by Thomas Rowlandson at left. The sword-carrying lieutenant (far left) wears a more elegant uniform than the midshipman (middle) with the sextant—and both are easily distinguished from the cabin boy with his bucket and mop. All three would have been found aboard the British frigate Charon, a section of whose gun deck (shown below) has been restored for display at Yorktown.

Cornwallis even wrote a letter asking Washington to care for his hospital cases.

The American cavalryman Henry "Light Horse Harry" Lee, who was at Yorktown, knew from his own experience in the South the risk involved in such a march. He later admired the daring of Cornwallis' plan: "This bold conception bespoke the hero, and was worthy of its author," Lee wrote in his memoirs. "Nor can it justly be deemed so desperate as was generally conceived."

Cornwallis knew that Washington would have to guard against two possible escape routes from Gloucester. The British could swing in a wide arc around Williamsburg and march through thinly populated western Virginia into North Carolina, or they could keep going toward New York. "Washington could not possibly in time seize the northern and the southern route; and without availing himself of horses, he could never overtake his foe," concluded Lee.

A moonless night enveloped the

Working from a bluff on the Gloucester side of the York River, the artist who painted this water color drew the siege precisely as he saw it. Thus, only the roofs of the dockside warehouses, and

broad river and the little towns on either side of it. While the allied guns continued to boom, Cornwallis began his last gamble. From Stephan Popp's regiment came three hundred Germans, who relieved the British light infantry in the hornwork. Down on the river the British veterans boarded sixteen big flatboats manned by sailors of the navy. In a few moments they were joined by the Royal Foot Guards and the Royal Welsh Fusiliers. These were the best troops in the army and Cornwallis wanted them to reach Gloucester early so that they could get as much sleep as possible before dawn.

On the Gloucester side, Colonel Tarleton ordered out extra guards of cavalry and infantry. Many officers served as temporary sentries to prevent any deserters or spies from slipping out to warn the enemy. The artillery and wagons were prepared, and infantrymen were assigned to every spare horse.

It took two hours for the cumbersome boats to make the first round

FROM THE SIMCOE PAPERS, COLONIAL WILLIAMSBURG

he masts and upper rigging of the ships tied up at them, are visible. In the middleground, the French fleet flies an outsize Tricolor only slightly smaller than the Union Jack over Yorktown.

trip across the river. The rest of the British army could only wait, while the shot crashed around them and the blazing mortar shells tumbled through the night. Sleep, young Popp recalled, "was something they had forgotten for a long time." Finally, at about midnight, the weary sailors arrived to pick up the second contingent.

Not a sign of alarm had come from the allied camp; on the river the sailors reported no patrol boats. The perimeter outside the Gloucester camp was equally silent. As he watched the second detachment pull away, Cornwallis must have thought that there was a chance of rescuing his army from this catastrophe after all.

Then scattered showers began to fall. Thunder from the sky muffled the man-made thunder from the allied lines, as a driving rain drummed upon the river. Jagged bolts of lightning gave the men on the shore an occasional glimpse of the soldiers and sailors, struggling to control the overloaded boats in the rising wind. Within five minutes a gale was churning the river. It was almost as violent as the storm that had surprised the British fleet in New York harbor.

For two full hours the storm raged. Wallowing in the swells, their sailors exhausted, all the boats were driven back to the Yorktown shore. Most were forced to land more than a mile below the town. (Two were blown four or five miles down the river, where they were captured at dawn by the French men-of-war at the mouth of the York.) On the Gloucester shore, Banastre Tarleton was still waiting, eager to begin the breakout operation. Instead of the second detachment, a lone boat appeared out of the darkness. A staff officer gave Tarleton a dismaying order: The Guards and light infantry were to return to Yorktown immediately.

The storm had devoured the precious darkness that Cornwallis needed in order to reorganize the second detachment, ferry it to Gloucester, and get the boats back again to York for the third detachment. There was nothing to do but to resume the weary business of the siege.

At dawn on October 17, the allied guns opened up with point-blank fury. During the night all the cannon had been shifted to batteries in the second parallel. From both flanks and from the center, one hundred muzzles belched death on the huddle of regiments and companies that once had been the proud British Army of Virginia. Walls crumbled under the terrific impact of the slamming round shot. Not a single British artilleryman dared to fire a gun in reply. The soldiers could do nothing now but suffer numbly.

In the hornwork, at about seven A.M., Cornwallis and Brigadier General Charles O'Hara morosely studied the overwhelming circle of bellowing guns. Then Cornwallis called a council of war. Only about one hundred mortar shells were left, reported Captain George Rochfort of the artillery,

Although the flags themselves have long since faded or frayed, most of the standards carried at Yorktown have been preserved in Gherardi Davis' faithful 1907 water colors. Among them are flags of four French units: the Soissonnais (top rear) and the Auxonne Artillery (top front), and below them, the flags from Metz (rear) and Dillon (front).

123

STATE COOKS, or
THE DOWNFALL of the FISH KETTLE.

Standing before a map of North America on which Yorktown is plainly marked, an English-man bemoans the overturned Colonial "fish kettle." A second official comforts him with the assurance that his Plan of Taxes, 1782, will somehow recoup British losses. Genuine con-fusion about the lost territory is evidenced by fish labeled "Nova Scotia" and "Quebec."

and not a single round of solid shot. The hospital was swamped with sick and wounded. A sleepless, heartsick Cornwallis asked his officers for advice. Should they fight to the last man?

The answer was *no*. Such an order would betray brave men who had done all that he had asked of them and more. There was only one decent alternative: immediate surrender. Before the end of the day, the dirt walls that were offering the men some slight protection might crumble entirely, exposing them to the enemy artillery. Already they were so exhausted and discouraged, their ranks so thinned by wounds and fever, that they could never hope to withstand an assault from veteran troops who outnumbered them by almost four to one. And that assault, the British officers knew, was certain to come within the next twenty-four hours.

Sadly, Cornwallis admitted that his officers were right. Turning to an aide, he dictated an historic letter to George Washington.

Sir, I propose a cessation of hostilities for twenty-four hours, and that two officers may be appointed by each side to meet at Mr. Moore's house to settle terms for the surrender of the posts at York and Gloucester

I have the honour to be &c.
Cornwallis

Cornwallis' October 17 request for a halt in the barrage while officers were appointed to discuss terms for the surrender of Yorktown and Gloucester was both brief and courteous.

8

"THE WORLD TURN'D

UPSIDE DOWN"

One of Yorktown's most dedicated diarists, Lieutenant Ebenezer Denny, was on duty in the American lines on the morning of October 17. A tour in the trenches by then had become rather routine and even a little boring to Denny and his fellow infantrymen. There was nothing to do but to watch the artillerymen work the guns. There were no further trenches to be dug and little or no return fire from inside Yorktown.

About nine o'clock the "monotony" was broken. A small red-coated figure appeared on the battered parapet in the center of the British works. He was beating vigorously on a drum.

"Had we not seen . . . the red coat when he first mounted," Denny wrote, "he might have beat till doomsday. The constant firing was too much for

For his Yorktown surrender scene, artist John Trumbull first made pencil sketches of individual officers (see page 99), then grouped them in oil sketches like the one at left. In the final version (pages 142–143), the central figure of Washington's second in command, Benjamin Lincoln, was faced front and given a plumed hat.

127

the sound of a single drum." Next a British officer waving a white handkerchief stepped calmly outside the hornwork and began walking toward the American lines. The drummerboy followed him, still pounding away.

Abruptly the allied guns ceased their thunder. Dazed by the sudden, unbelievable silence, the men for the first time heard the sound of the drummerboy beating a signal that the French call a *chamade.* "I thought I never heard a drum equal to it," Denny recalled, "the most delightful music to us all." An American officer met the Britons halfway. He tied the white surrender handkerchief over the British officer's eyes. The drummerboy went back to Yorktown, and the Englishman walked into the American trenches, where he handed over Cornwallis' letter.

A messenger rushed the letter to George Washington's tent. The commander in chief immediately prepared a reply. He told Cornwallis that he had "an ardent desire" to prevent any further "effusion of blood." But before he would agree to negotiate, he wanted a summary of the terms that Cornwallis expected. Washington was not going to let the British use up precious time making outrageous demands that he could not possibly grant. He would give Cornwallis two hours to state these terms. For that time, and not a moment longer, the bombardment would cease.

While Washington and his aides composed this letter, the allied can-

non went back to work on Yorktown. They continued to pound away until two o'clock in the afternoon, when the Americans ran up a flag of truce and delivered Washington's answer to Cornwallis. The guns remained silent during the next two hours, as Washington had promised.

At about the same time, in New York, the British fleet was finally getting under way. Reaching the open sea proved to be a slow business, however. When night came, three ships of the line were still in the Hudson River.

At Yorktown, while Cornwallis weighed Washington's reply, the two armies confronted each other in unaccustomed silence. In the hornwork, Stephan Popp realized for the first time that surrender was close. The British light infantrymen began to slash their tents and deliberately destroy their equipment. In the American lines, men laughed when they suddenly remembered that the date was October 17—the same day on which General John Burgoyne had surrendered another British army at Saratoga in 1777. It was, Sergeant Joseph Plumb Martin cheerfully noted, "a rather unlucky day for the British."

Cornwallis resented Washington's insistence on written terms of surrender within two hours. Still hoping for the appearance of Clinton's relief fleet on the horizon, the British commander was quite frankly stalling for time. But with those French and American cannon staring down his throat, he had no choice. His reply stated the

A British army drummerboy

George Tucker wrote: "A solemn stillness prevailed—the night was remarkably clear & the sky decorated with ten thousand stars—numberless Meteors gleaming thro' the Atmosphere afforded a pleasing resemblance to the Bombs which had exhibited, a noble Firework the night before, but happily divested of all their Horror."

At dawn on the eighteenth, unfamiliar music came drifting from the British lines—at first harsh to French and American ears. Scottish bagpipers, no doubt from the Seventy-sixth Regiment, were saluting the enemy. Proudly, the Royal Deux-Ponts Regimental Band replied through the grey stillness. The rising sun slowly revealed a remarkable sight. On both sides of the lines the parapets were crowded with men and officers. No one shouted insults or waved defiant fists. The soldiers simply gazed at the gouged, littered battlefield, as if for the first time they were seeing the ugly face of war.

During the night, Washington had labored over a detailed reply to the surrender terms. He bluntly rejected Cornwallis' request to send his army back to Europe as paroled prisoners. With minor exceptions, Washington agreed to the rest of Cornwallis' proposals. He closed his letter with the urgent suggestion that the British General appoint commissioners to draw up a formal surrender, "or a renewal of hostilities may take place." Once more Washington gave the British only two hours to reach a decision.

terms that he expected to receive and added, hopefully, that he would have no objection to a "continuance" of the truce.

Washington may have smiled at this last remark. Certainly the British wanted the cannon to remain silent, far more than did the allies. After glancing at the terms and finding nothing that was seriously objectionable, Washington agreed. He knew that he had won.

Silence, if not authentic peace, descended on Yorktown. That night men on both sides of the lines could sleep—for the first time in eight days —without wondering if a mortar shell or a cannon ball would kill them before they awoke. In his diary St.

In the American commander's mind was always the fear that de Grasse's departure or the return of the British fleet might snatch away this vital victory at the last moment.

Washington might have been a little more lenient about time if he had known where the British fleet was when he sent his answer to Cornwallis. On October 18, the remaining men-of-war finally left the Hudson River and sailed through the Narrows toward the sea. Yet another fine day, with moderate wind, was wasted in transferring the troops from the transports to the men-of-war off Sandy Hook. Only four ships went over the bar and actually reached the open waters of the Atlantic that day.

In Yorktown, Cornwallis read Washington's terms and unhappily agreed to "appoint two field officers from my army to meet two officers from you at any time and place that you think proper, to digest the articles of capitulation."

The Augustine Moore house, half a mile behind the American first parallel, was chosen as a site for the commissioners' conference. Washington gave Colonel John Laurens the coveted honor of acting as his representative and asked Rochambeau to select a French officer to accompany him. The French General chose the Vicomte de Noailles, no doubt as a reward for his work in repelling the predawn British sortie two days earlier. Cornwallis appointed his aide, Major Alexander Ross, and Lieutenant Colonel Thomas Dundas.

Over on the Gloucester side, the Duc de Lauzun was ordered to discuss details with his personal antagonist, Banastre Tarleton. The Duke advanced to the parley waving a white lace handkerchief, thus maintaining the well-established tradition, stated

by a fellow Frenchman, "that the Duc de Lauzun never acted like anyone else would in the same circumstances."

Laurens and Noailles met the British commissioners in the small parlor of the Moore house on the afternoon of October 18, 1781. John Laurens wore his simple buff and blue American uniform, and Noailles was splendid in his French uniform of white and gold. The two red-coated British officers may have looked a bit bedraggled from spending their nights in Yorktown's caves. As officers and gentlemen, they were greeted by Laurens and Noailles with grave courtesy.

Most people thought that the negotiations would last only a few hours. The commanders had apparently decided the major points. Washington ordered a four-hundred-man detachment, half American, half French, to be ready to occupy Yorktown before nightfall. But the afternoon faded without a sign of the commissioners or the surrender articles.

Major Ross and Colonel Laurens were arguing vitriolically over how the defeated army would march out. According to the traditional rules of siege warfare in the eighteenth century, if a commander surrendered a fortress before the place was taken by storm, and he had put up a strong defense, he was allowed to march out with "the honors of war." This meant that his men kept their swords and guns to protect themselves against insults, and the army kept all its regimental and national flags flying boldly.

Trumbull's superb study of the surrender is actually a composite, pieced together over an eleven-year period—from 1786 to 1797—out of sketches made on both sides of the Atlantic. This lovely panorama of the battlefield, showing the Augustine Moore house (left), where the articles of capitulation were drawn up, was included in the background of Trumbull's final canvas.

At Cornwallis' suggestion, the articles of capitulation were drafted at the Augustine Moore house (above), located just behind the first allied siege line, on October 18. Expecting a rapid settlement, the allies were surprised when the talks dragged on well into the evening.

His bands could play one of the victor's national songs. Saluting the enemy with his own music was a way of saying that the defeated army was still strong and proud enough to exchange compliments.

Laurens sternly refused to concede any of these privileges to the British.

He had been captured at Charleston in 1780, and he had never forgotten that the British had refused such honors to the trapped Americans under Major General Benjamin Lincoln when they finally surrendered.

Ross protested this polite revenge. "This is a harsh article," he said.

"Which article?" asked Laurens.

"The troops shall march out with colors cased and drums beating a British or a German march."

"Yes, sir," replied Laurens, "it is a harsh article."

"Then, Colonel Laurens, if that is your opinion, why is it here?"

With superb formality, Laurens answered: "Your question, Major Ross, compels an observation which I would have gladly suppressed. You seem to forget, sir, that I was a capitulant at Charleston, where General Lincoln, after a brave defense of six weeks in open trenches by a very inconsiderable garrison against the British army and fleet . . . and when your lines of approach were within pistol shot of our field works, was refused any other terms for his gallant garrison than marching out with colors cased and drums *not* beating a German or a British march."

"But," said Major Ross, "My Lord Cornwallis did not command at Charleston."

"There, sir," said Laurens, "you extort another declaration. It is not the individual that is here considered. It is the nation. This remains an article, or I cease to be a commissioner."

Ross gave up and tried to get the honors of war for the garrison of Gloucester, at least. He pointed out that except for the skirmish between Lauzun and Tarleton, scarcely a shot had been fired at them. Laurens refused to relent. Gloucester and Yorktown were all one garrison, he insisted.

But Ross wore him down, and Laurens finally agreed to let Tarleton's cavalry ride out of Gloucester with drawn swords and blaring trumpets. However, the infantry would have to march out with colors cased.

It was almost midnight before the haggling over these and other points ended. Even then, the weary Laurens and Noailles returned to Washington's tent with only a rough draft of the articles of capitulation. Before they parted, the commissioners had agreed to extend the truce until nine o'clock on the morning of the nineteenth. The men of both armies enjoyed a second peaceful night.

By morning, the articles were in final form and were presented to Washington for his approval or rejection. He accepted them with only minor alterations and had the whole document copied. A messenger rushed one copy to the British commander. In a separate note, Washington told Cornwallis that he wanted to have everything signed by eleven o'clock. At two o'clock the garrison was expected to march out for the formal surrender ceremonies.

After breakfast, Washington rode out to the captured British redoubt number ten, where he was joined by Rochambeau and Admiral Barras (acting for de Grasse, who was ill). Other high-ranking officers waited impatiently nearby while Cornwallis studied the terms in a Yorktown cave.

Off Sandy Hook, at about the same hour, the British fleet was finally at

Cows now graze in the field where, on October 19, 1781, surrendering regiments of dispirited British

JACK NEWMAN

nd German troops laid down their weapons after Cornwallis had signed the articles of capitulation.

sea. Somehow, Sir Henry Clinton had talked himself into a very optimistic mood. In a letter to a friend in England, he said that Cornwallis' position was impregnable. Although he understood "nothing of [naval] matters," he thought that they had an excellent chance of defeating the French fleet and joining Cornwallis to do battle with George Washington's American army.

More than once, while Cornwallis studied Washington's terms, his eyes must have turned to the broad river, and beyond it, to the open bay, hoping to see on the horizon the masts of the British fleet. But the only thing he saw were the masts of the French men-of-war riding at anchor in the mouth of the York. Only minutes before Washington's deadline, Cornwallis reluctantly put his signature at the bottom of the surrender articles. Captain Thomas Symonds signed beneath for the British navy.

An aide then delivered the documents to redoubt number ten, where the American commander in chief wrote "G. Washington" for the Americans. For the French, there was "Le Comte de Rochambeau" and Barras: " *Le Comte de Barras en mon nom & celui du Comte de Grasse.*" No whoops of victory sounded from the watching officers and men. They followed Washington's example of quiet dignity.

The commander in chief finally ordered an aide to place above the allied signatures the line: "Done in the trenches before Yorktown in Virginia,

October 19, 1781." Then he rode calmly back to his tent.

Not everyone in the American ranks was as composed as Washington. An incident in the actual takeover of Yorktown revealed the tensions of the day. Baron von Steuben headed the American detachment that marched in to occupy Yorktown. Among the soldiers was Lieutenant Ebenezer Denny, who had been given the honor of planting the regimental standard on the British parapet. But the Baron had no intention of letting a mere lieutenant perform this victorious flourish.

As Denny mounted the parapet, Steuben grabbed the flag out of his hand and personally shoved the pole into the dirt. Colonel Richard Butler, the commander of Denny's regiment, almost shot von Steuben on the spot. He and the Baron exchanged vivid insults, while friends of both men watched in dismay.

Conditions inside Yorktown disgusted young Denny. "Never was in so filthy a place—some handsome houses, but prodigiously shattered. Negroes lie about sick and dying, in every stage of the small pox. Vast heaps of shot and shells which came from our works."

In spite of this chaos all around them, the British were determined to

The part of the surrender articles that Washington and two of the French commanders signed has been lost, and only the names of the British capitulants remain (right).

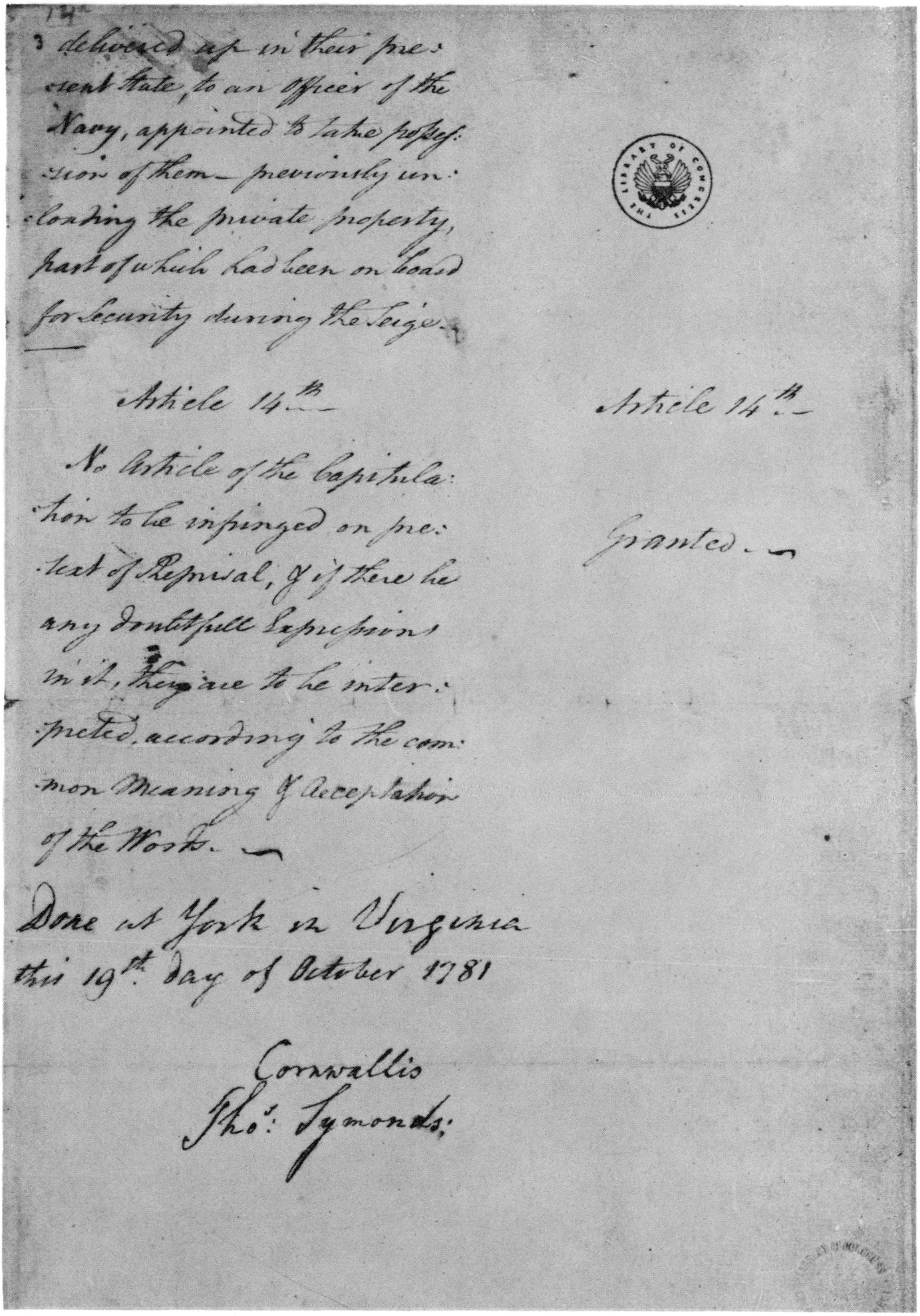

3 delivered up in their pre:
:sent State, to an Officer of the
Navy, appointed to take posses:
:sion of them — previously un:
:loading the private property,
part of which had been on board
for Security during the Seige. —

Article 14th —

No Article of the Capitula:
:tion to be infringed on pre:
:text of Reprisal, & if there be
any doubtfull Expressions
in it, they are to be inter:
:preted according to the com:
:mon Meaning & Acceptation
of the Words. —

Article 14th —

Granted —

Done at York in Virginia
this 19th day of October 1781

Cornwallis
Thos. Symonds.

MANUSCRIPT DIVISION, LIBRARY OF CONGRESS

Although the Thirty-third Foot was one of the British infantry units defeated at Yorktown, its flag (above) was not among those surrendered. For some reason, the banner had been left behind in New York.

look their best for the surrender ceremonies. The soldiers were ordered to shine their boots and whiten their gaiters. Fresh uniforms were distributed from the army stores. The commissary department also was generous with its reserve supplies of rum, letting the soldiers fill their canteens with this favorite army drink.

The French and the Americans were sprucing for the big show too. The French broke out their best uniforms, and the officers put on all their plumes and gold braid. The Americans polished their guns and boots and repaired their threadbare uni-

forms as much as possible. For the surrender site Washington had selected a meadow about a half mile down the Hampton road from the inner British defense lines.

At about one P.M. the French and American regiments marched out of their camps and lined up along the road. The Americans stationed the Continentals in the front ranks and put the militia, with their sloppy civilian clothes and unmilitary manners, behind them. The French did not have to worry about such problems and simply formed up, rank after glittering rank, on the other side of the road, facing the Americans.

Washington and his staff, all on horseback, rode to the head of the American column. Opposite them, also on horseback, were Rochambeau and his staff.

From the second parallel to where the generals waited, the combined armies formed a long military lane. In the field behind them was a throng of civilians, some on foot, others in wagons and chaises.

For a while the French regimental bands enlivened the waiting with martial music. Then they ceased, and from Yorktown came the beat of drums, pounding a slow march, and band instruments playing a mournful tune. The British were marching out.

First came a handsome officer in full dress, followed by an equally splendid staff. Eyes strained, necks craned for a look at the "southern Hannibal," Cornwallis. But the Brit-

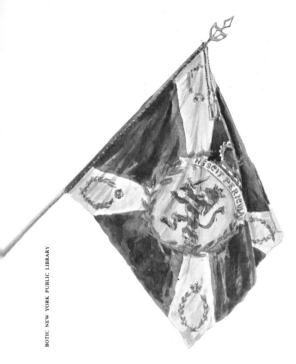

Like the English flag opposite (and the French regimental colors on page 123), the unidentified Hessian battle flag above was drawn by American water colorist Gherardi Davis and published early in this century.

ish commander had discovered, at the last moment, that he could not endure the pain of the surrender. The leading horseman was Brigadier General Charles O'Hara. As the British entered the twin rows of the allied army, many Americans recognized the tune that their bands were playing. Dozens of songs and ballads had been written to the familiar notes. One was called "When the King Enjoys His Own Again." A better-known version was "The World Turn'd Upside Down."

The Americans naturally preferred the latter version. They were keenly aware that these soldiers of the world's most powerful king were surrendering to tattered rebels who had defied imperial power in the name of a new idea, a nation conceived in liberty. The British knew this too, and their conduct made it plain that Cornwallis was not the only one who found this surrender painful. As their ranks marched past, every English soldier riveted his eyes to the right, at the French, deliberately ignoring the Americans on the other side of the road.

Lafayette declined to tolerate this final insult. He barked an order, and the American band burst into its favorite song, "Yankee Doodle." The explosion of fifes and drums jerked every British head in the other direction. Against their will, they stared into the faces of the colonials whom they had so long scorned and despised.

Meanwhile, at the head of the British column, General O'Hara spurred his horse toward General Rochambeau. The Comte Mathieu Dumas saw that O'Hara was following the same policy of studied insult and wanted to surrender to the French, not the Americans. The young aide thrust his horse between O'Hara and Rochambeau. Simultaneously, the French General shook his head and pointed across the road to Washington.

O'Hara produced a glittering, if somewhat embarrassed, smile and introduced himself to the allied commander in chief. Lord Cornwallis was indisposed, he said, and he was acting in his place. Washington demonstrated that he knew his military protocol by

139

calmly telling O'Hara to take his orders from Major General Benjamin Lincoln, the American second in command.

Lincoln explained the line of march to the surrender field, where a detachment of French hussars had formed a circle. The British were to pile their guns within the circle, execute an about-face, and return to Yorktown.

The red-coated ranks marched toward the circle of hussars. Not a scornful or insulting word was spoken by either French or Americans. Everyone, even the Americans, suddenly felt sorry for these beaten soldiers, now that they were no longer enemies.

As each platoon reached the hussars, the sergeant gave the bitter order: "Ground arms!" One American thought that in most cases the order was given "sullenly"—which is not surprising. At first, many men hurled their muskets to the ground as violently as possible, hoping to damage them. But a curt warning from General Lincoln quickly stopped their defiant action.

The sight of the army abandoning its weapons was almost unbearable for many officers. Some, mostly English, swore terrible oaths. Lieutenant Colonel Abercromby is reported to have bitten his sword in mortification. Tears streamed openly down other cheeks. A Scot in the Seventy-sixth Regiment hugged his gun the way a lover embraces his sweetheart and flung it down, crying, "May you never get so good a master!" Only the German mercenaries performed the operation without emotion.

The surrendered muskets were a huge brown and silver pile by the time the last German platoon had laid down its guns and marched away, and by three o'clock the British were back in Yorktown. On the Gloucester side the surrender ceremony was just beginning. Tarleton's troopers rode

Stalking off (right foreground) after laying down their rifles, the two British soldiers in this 1785 German wash drawing typify the captured army's bitter attitude.

out with their sabers drawn, their trumpets defiantly braying, taking every possible advantage of the surrender terms. The infantry marched with colors cased, their drums beating an unidentified English march.

Both the Americans and the French now rushed to extend every courtesy to the captured British officers. Washington invited General O'Hara to dinner that night. The French entertained other English officers and lent them money and clothing. The British were especially amazed at the treatment they received from the French, their traditional enemies. Captain Samuel Graham said that he was "overwhelmed" by the French expressions of sympathy.

Only when they were alone did the Americans celebrate. That night one American colonel wrote: "I noticed that the officers and soldiers could scarcely talk for laughing and they could scarcely walk for jumping and dancing and singing. . . ."

For the men on duty inside Yorktown the hours after the surrender were not so pleasant. In the defeated army, discipline collapsed. The enlisted men got drunk on their rum-filled canteens and spent the night brawling and looting. Three times they tried to break into the captured stores and were stopped by Lieutenant Denny and his men. One drunken redcoat went berserk and killed an American with a bayonet. The redcoat, in turn, no doubt became Yorktown's last casualty.

Yorktown was a comparatively bloodless victory, considering the number of men involved. The British army had 156 killed, 326 wounded, and 70 missing, a total of 552 casualties. American casualties were about 30 dead and 100 wounded—an estimate, because militia losses were not recorded. The French lost 60 killed and 193 wounded, for an allied total of 383. Disease had cut down far more men on both sides. More than 3,500 soldiers were in hospitals when Cornwallis surrendered.

Washington gave his aide Colonel Tench Tilghman—who had served with him since 1776—the honor of bearing the victory dispatch to the Continental Congress. Hiring boats and horses, Tilghman made the trip to Philadelphia in two days.

After presenting the General's momentous message to the President of the Congress, Colonel Tilghman asked for money to pay for the expenses of his trip. The Congress was mortified to confess that there was not one dollar in the national treasury.

OVERLEAF: *John Trumbull's final version of the surrender scene is a good deal more formal than most of his early sketches. General Benjamin Lincoln leads a group of unidentified British officers between near-symmetrical ranks of allied officers. The latter include Lauzun and Rochambeau (left, fore and rear, on prancing horses), and Knox and Washington (right, fore and rear, directly opposite their French allies). Alexander Hamilton is third from right.*

141

Finally, each member dug a dollar in hard money out of his own pocket, and Yorktown's messenger of victory was rescued from possible arrest for debt.

A few days later, off the capes of Virginia, the British flagship *London*, part of the fleet from New York, sighted a small boat. In it were a white man and two Negroes. From them Admiral Graves and General Clinton learned the grim news that Yorktown had surrendered. The fleet cruised off the mouth of the Chesapeake for five more days. Other loyalist refugees who trickled out in rowboats and sloops confirmed the first report. Cornwallis and his men were prisoners. One third of the British army in America was lost.

On the sixteenth of November the frigate *Lively* arrived in London with news that Cornwallis was trapped and that the fleet and army were about to sail from New York to rescue him.

The British capital spent nine days in anguished suspense, talking of little else. On the evening of the twenty-fifth, a Sunday, Captain Melcome, commander of His Majesty's sloop *Rattlesnake*, entered the Admiralty offices with dispatches from Admiral Graves. Written off the Virginia capes, these dispatches reported the sad news Graves had learned from Yorktown's loyalist refugees.

Lord Germain, Secretary of State for Colonies, was promptly informed. He waited until the next morning to tell the King's chief minister, Lord North. Both men knew what the disaster meant.

"Oh God," Lord North said, pacing up and down his apartment at 10 Downing Street. "It is all over. It is all over."

In America, this was by no means evident. Nathanael Greene had to spend two more months of hard fighting to clear the British from the interior of Georgia and South Carolina, and Washington hurried back to guard the British army in New York. De Grasse was caught by a revived British fleet and badly beaten in the West Indies in April, 1782. Captain William Cornwallis, brother of the defeated General, commanded the man-of-war that captured the unlucky Frenchman and his flagship.

Yet Great Britain was sick of the war. On March 5, 1782, Parliament had voted for peace, and American negotiators, led by Benjamin Franklin, began a long series of meetings with British and French diplomats. A preliminary peace treaty was signed on November 30, 1782, and a final treaty on September 3, 1783. Only then did men have time to look back and realize that Yorktown was the blow that broke the British will to win and enabled the Americans to insist on independence.

Overjoyed Americans responded to the news of Cornwallis' surrender with broadsides such as this one, which was published in Boston in 1782. Readers are urged to sing it to "the merriest Tunes you can find."

GREAT JOY
TO THE
DAY.

WASHINGTON.
AND
COUNT DE GRASSE:
A NEW SONG,

Designed to add Mirth to the Day of General Thanksgiving, Rejoicing and Illumi-
nation, on Account of the late great and glorious News of the taking York-Town, in
Virginia, in which were Lord Cornwallis and a large Knot of British troops, &c. said
to be 9000 in the whole; with a 40 gun ship, a frigate, an arm'd sloop and 100 transports.

[☞ Tune of WASHINGTON, or any one of the merriest Tunes you can find.]

COME jolly brave AMERICANS, and toss the glass around,
Unto those worthy PATRIOTS who rule in Camp or Town;
Unto our Great Commander brave glorious WASHINGTON,
To COUNT DE GRASSE and General GREENE and ev'ry Patriot Son.

GOD bless our valiant WASHINGTON! and may he long survive,
Till he compleats a victory o'er all his foes alive;
May Heaven's blessings each descend, unitedly engage
To crown his life with happiness unto a good old age.

Let all who love AMERICA, in all their sonnets sing
The late exploits of COUNT DE GRASSE and warlike General GREENE
And may each true AMERICAN those valiant SONS adore,
For all their brave heroic deeds 'till time shall be no more.

O what a noble capture 'twas! must ev'ry one confess,
Of valiant COUNT DE GRASSE of late, and each the Hero bless;
His conqu'ring pow'r by sea display'd, forc'd British ships to strike,
One hundred sail of transports yield to the Blue and White:

Besides three British men of war were captur'd by his hand,
Struck to this noble ADMIRAL'S flag, and bow'd at his command.
Nine thousand of their armed troops were conquer'd all in one,
Huzza! for Admiral COUNT DE GRASSE and glorious WASHINGTON.

GOD bless our noble GOVERNOR! long may he yet survive,
A scourge to all base Tories who wickedly connive
To undermine fair FREEDOM's walls, with all her noble train;
Huzza! for all our PATRIOT SONS, let FREEDOM ever reign.

Sold at RUSSELL's Printing-Office, near Liberty-Stump. (Pr. 4 Cop.) ☞ At the same Place may be
had, cheap to Travelling-traders, &c. BICKERSTAFF's BOSTON ALMANACK for 1782.

Working from existing portraits, Benjamin West had blocked in the figures and nearly finished the faces of the five American delegates to the 1783 London peace conference when he learned that the British commissioners had refused to pose for him. West was left with nearly finished portraits of (left to right): John Jay, John Adams, Benjamin Franklin, Henry Laurens, and Franklin's grandson, William Temple Franklin—and no way of filling the rest of the canvas.

147

Continental scrip (above) was so drastically devalued by 1781 that any useless item was said to be "not worth a continental."

AMERICAN HERITAGE JUNIOR LIBRARY

JOSEPH L. GARDNER, *Editor*

Janet Czarnetzki, *Art Director*

Sandra L. Russell, *Copy Editor*

Laurie P. Phillips, *Picture Editor*

Kathleen Fitzpatrick, *Assistant Copy Editor*

Edwin D. Bayrd, Jr., *Editorial Assistant*

ACKNOWLEDGMENTS

The Editors are particularly grateful for the assistance of the following individuals and organizations:

Michael Blow

Anne S. K. Brown Military Collection, Providence, Rhode Island—Richard B. Harrington

William L. Clements Library, University of Michigan—Nathaniel N. Shipton

Henry E. Huntington Library and Art Gallery, San Marino, California—Mrs. Barbara Boucot

Library of Congress—Milton Kaplan, Gayle Thornbrough

Mariners Museum, Newport News, Virginia

Mount Vernon Ladies' Association of the Union

Morristown National Historical Park, Morristown, New Jersey—Theodore C. Sowers

Norfolk Museum of Arts and Sciences, Norfolk, Virginia—Henry Caldwell, Phil Morrison

FURTHER REFERENCE

Working with scrupulous accuracy over a period of many years, the National Park Service has restored most of the Revolutionary roads, buildings, and fortifications at the Yorktown battle site and—after exhaustive research—reconstructed many others. Thus, today's visitor to the Colonial National Historical Park in Virginia is able to survey, from the observation deck of the visitors' center, the rebuilt redoubts, complete with their protective palisades and menacing abatis (see page 75). In addition, a Park Service tour of the battlements and town provides a chance to inspect the cave in which Cornwallis spent the final hours of the siege, sheltered from allied fire, as well as the field headquarters of the French and American commanders and the surrender field itself (see pages 134–135). Those readers who are unable to visit the park but wish to learn more about the Battle of Yorktown should read *Beat the Last Drum: The Siege of Yorktown, 1781* (St. Martin's Press, 1963), a volume in which Thomas J. Fleming, the author of this work, examines the same historic events in greater depth for an adult audience. Other recommended works on Yorktown and the American Revolution include:

Flexner, James T., *George Washington and the American Revolution.* Little, Brown, 1968.

Freeman, Douglas Southall, *Victory with the Help of France* (*George Washington*, Vol. V). Scribner's, 1952.

Ketchum, Richard M., ed., *The American Heritage Book of the Revolution.* American Heritage, 1958.

Larrabee, Harold A., *Decision at the Chesapeake.* Clarkson N. Potter, 1964.

Mahan, A. T., *Major Operations of the Navies in the War of American Independence.* Sampson Low, 1913.

Willcox, William B., *Portrait of a General: Sir Henry Clinton in the War of Independence.* Knopf, 1964.

INDEX

Boldface indicates pages on which maps or illustrations appear

A

Abercromby, Lt. Col. Robert, 112–113, 115, 140

Army, British, 14, 16, 17, 24, 26–37 *passim*
life and conditions in, 7, 28, 63, **63**, 64, **64**, 110–118, 139
operations and campaigns of: New York, 14, 17, 20, 22–23, 24, **24–25**, 26, 29, 31, 41, 73, 144; Philadelphia, 26; South, 28–29; Georgia, 12, 29, 144; North Carolina, 29, 31; South Carolina, 12–13, 25, 28, 29, 31, 32–33, 144; Virginia (other than Yorktown), 7, 13–14, 22, 25, 31, 34, 35; West Indies, **22–23**, 26
operations and campaigns at Yorktown and Gloucester, Va. (Yorktown campaign): fortification of, 25, 35, 37, 38, 44, 50, 52, 53; defense of, 59, 61–73, **66**, **72–73**, 74, 76, 86–95 *passim*, 110–118; counterattack and sortie at, 106–107, 112–115; breakout attempt at Gloucester and retreat to Yorktown, 115–125 *passim*; surrender of, **title page**, 7, 8, **126–127**, 128–141, **140**, **142–143**, **back endsheet**; casualties in, 91, 95, 115, 118, 120, 125, 141
units of, in Yorktown and Gloucester campaign: cavalry, 69–70, 118, 121; infantry, 35, 91, 121, 122, 128, 138, 141; German, 62, 65, 66, 91, 94, 105, 106–109, 118, 121, 135, 140; Hessian, 62, 91, 94, 95, 106–107, 139; Royal Foot Guards, 121–122; Royal Welsh Fusiliers, 62, 65, 69–70, 98, 101, 121; Scottish Highlanders, 62; Seventy-sixth Regiment, 129, 140

Army, Continental, 11, 22, 50
flags and equipment of, **6**, 7, 8, **89**, 92–93, **92–93**, **back cover**
life and conditions in, 7, 13–14, 22–23, 43, 53, 55, 56, 58, 64, 71, 73, 87, 99, 104, 108
Negroes in, 19, 23
uniforms of, 19–20, 59, **59**, 71, **71**, 92–93, **92–93**, 138
operations and campaigns of: New York, 19–20, 22, 24–25, 26, 29, 31, 40–41; North Carolina, 31; South Carolina, 12–13, 25, 29, 31, **32–33**, 144; Virginia (before Yorktown), 14, 31, 34, 35
en route to Yorktown, 38, 43–44, 50, 52, 58–59; in New Jersey, 40–41; in Philadelphia, 43; in Williamsburg, 45, 56
operations in Yorktown and Gloucester campaign: siege of, 59, 61–73, **71**, 79, **96–97**, 97; bombardment of, 82–83, 85, 88–95, 122, 128; assault on, 97–109, 113, **113**; cessation of fighting, 129; and surrender ceremonies, **126–127**, 138, 139–141, **140**, **142–143**, **back endsheet**; occupation of Yorktown, 131, 136; casualties of, 88, 106, 141
units of, in Yorktown and Gloucester campaign: artillery, 58, 71, 73, 82, 88, 91, 94–95, 98, 106, 108–109, 112–115 *passim*, 122; cavalry, 59; Continental Line, 70; infantry, 58, **58**, 59, 77, 79, 100–101, 102–103, 105, 109; Pennsylvania Line, 70, 107–108; sappers and miners, 56, 74, 76–77, 86, 101, 102–

104; Virginia militia, 70, 85, 88, 113

Army, French, flags and equipment of, 8, 123, **123**, 139
life and conditions in, 7, 19, 40, 43, 53
uniforms of, **18**, 19–20
operations of (before Yorktown): departure from Brest, 12, **12–13**; in Newport, R.I., 13, 14, 17, **17**, 38; in New York, 17, 19–20
en route to Yorktown: 43–44, 52, 58–59; in New Jersey, 40–41; in Philadelphia, 43; in Williamsburg, 45, 50, 56
operations in Yorktown and Gloucester campaign: first battles of, 59, 65, 67; siege of, 70–73, **72–73**, 74–95 *passim*; bombardment of, 82–83, 85, 88–95 *passim*, 98; assault on, 97–109 *passim*; cessation of fighting, 129; and surrender ceremonies, 138–141, **142–143**; occupation of Yorktown, 131; casualties in, 88, 107, 108, 141
units of, in Yorktown and Gloucester campaign: artillery, 79, 82, 83, 88, 91, 94–95, 101, 112, 128; cavalry, 69–70; engineers, 74, 76, 77, 86; grenadiers and chasseurs, 99, 106, 107, 115; infantry, 109

Arnold, Benedict, 13, 41
effigy of, 100, **100**
and New London massacre, 101

B

Barras, Admiral Comte de, 38, 44, 50
and relief for allies at Yorktown, 38–40, 42, 43, 61, 63
at Yorktown surrender ceremonies,

Included in the French log book from which the drawing of the luckless French frigate Zélé *was taken (pages 56–57) is this unique pano-*

rama of the crucial naval battle of September 5, 1781. The British fleet (above) exchanges broadsides with the French fleet below it.